Love Crazy

By Allan Zullo

with Kathryn Zullo

ANDREWS AND MCMEEL • *A Universal Press Syndicate Company* • KANSAS CITY

Designed by Rick Cusick
Illustrations by Paul Coker

Library of Congress Cataloging-in-Publication Data

Zullo, Allan.
     Love crazy : outrageous but true stories of how couples met and married / by Allan Zullo with Kathryn Zullo.
          p. cm.
     ISBN 0-8362-1049-2 (pb)
     1. Man-woman relationships. 2. Dating (Social customs) 3. Marriage proposals.
I. Zullo, Kathryn. II. Title.
HQ801.Z85 1996
306.73—dc20   95-44566
                                                                    CIP

ATTENTION: SCHOOLS AND BUSINESSES
Andrews and McMeel books are available at quantity discounts with bulk purchase for educational, business, or sales promotional use. For information, please write to: Special Sales Department, Andrews and McMeel, 4900 Main Street, Kansas City, Missouri 64112.

Dedication

To Skeeter and Bubba,
  still crazy after all these years.

Contents

A Crazy Little Thing Called Love

SHAKESPEARE ONCE WROTE,

"We that are true lovers run into strange capers."

Strange, wacky, and silly capers. That's what happens when you fall deeply, madly, passionately in love. You do outrageous things that often defy logic—which is exactly what this book celebrates.

When you're madly in love, it doesn't matter that you weigh 125 pounds and the groom crushes the scales at nearly 1,000 pounds. Or that you stand six feet six inches tall, and your bride can't reach four feet on her tiptoes. So what if your wife is eighty-five years old and you're only nineteen? Or that you gave up the boring life of an English housewife to marry a Masai warrior and live in a mud hut in Africa?

When you lose your heart, love knows no time, no age. That's why you can track down your true love from sixty years ago, discover that the embers are still burning, and end up marrying him. And that's why, after divorcing forty years ago, you both realize you still love each other and remarry.

When you cherish your sweetheart, you conjure up clever ways to ask for your beloved's hand in marriage. You're a policeman—have her arrested and pop the question in her jail cell. You're a sportscaster—propose on the air in front of 40 million TV viewers. You're creative—ask her to marry you in a film you show at the movie theater.

When love isn't incredible enough, fate often is. You found your future mate after years of being strangers who waved to each other in passing cars. You found romance after misdialing a long-distance number and reaching a beautiful voice 750 miles away. And you found your future doctor and husband after accidentally falling down an elevator shaft.

Let's face it. You'll do anything for love. You'll get married in the back of a garbage truck in a gown made of trash bags and spend your wedding night in a landfill. You'll exchange "I do's" while standing knee-deep in a mud pit or hanging from a tree or running a marathon. You'll wed in a burning building, in a mine shaft, and even in virtual reality.

Yes, you'll do most anything because you're love crazy!

Dates with Destiny

Sleepless since Seattle

In a real-life version of the hit movie *Sleepless in Seattle*, two lost souls found each other and true love.

It all began in 1994 during a brief encounter in a lounge area at the Seattle-Tacoma International Airport. Barry Aurich, thirty, was waiting for a flight back to his home in Eugene, Oregon, while Rita Weddle, thirty-two, was waiting to return to her home in Yakima, Washington.

"He smiled and started chatting with me in a friendly way and I was caught up in the conversation," recalled Rita, a sales representative who had never been married. "We talked about hobbies, travel, everything under the sun. He told me about his divorce and the two young sons he was raising on his own. I felt like we had been friends forever."

After their engaging fifteen-minute chat, Barry left to catch his flight. "He turned back and gave me a smile," she recalled. "When he was gone, I missed him. I had felt close to him."

Barry said that when he sat in the plane, "I kept thinking, 'I've been looking for you so long. Am I ever going to see you again?'"

Back home that night, Barry tossed and turned in bed. He couldn't keep the sweet, engaging woman out of his mind. He just had to see her again. The only problem was that he forgot to get her name. He figured there was one way to find her—a newspaper ad.

The next morning, while thinking of the similarities between his situation and the storyline of the film *Sleepless in Seattle,* Barry composed an ad. He placed it in the *Yakima Herald-Republic,* asking readers to help him find the woman of his dreams. The ad, in the personals column, read: "SLEEPLESS SINCE SEATTLE! I left without even getting her name. Please help me find a woman I met at SeaTac Airport Tuesday night. She moved back to Yakima a year ago after living in Boston 5 years. She's 32, tall, slender, light brown/blonde straight hair, brown eyes, has several dogs & cats, never been married & works in financial planning field. If you know who she is, please have her call Barry in Eugene." The ad included his phone number.

The day the ad appeared, a friend of Rita's saw it and immediately called her to tell her about it. Rita was stunned. "I couldn't believe Barry was as attracted to me as I was to him," she recalled. "I phoned my mom for her advice. She said, 'Go for it. He sounds like one in a million.'"

The next day, Rita called Barry and they talked for three hours. They were soon gabbing most every day until Rita visited Barry. They took a camping trip together and fell in love.

"We talked until dawn under the stars and decided we couldn't live without each other," Rita recalled. "We kissed for the first time and the world stopped. It was perfect."

Less than three months later, they were married. "I believe everyone has a soulmate," said Rita. "If you look long enough, you'll find your true partner in life."

Driven Together by Fate

Every workday for five years, a handsome stranger in a green Chevelle waved to a pretty woman in a car going in the opposite direction.

Little did they know that one day they would wind up married to each other. Today Ray and Mary Ann Faulkner marvel at how fate drove them together.

In 1971, after another argument with her previous husband, Mary Ann, then a thirty-one-year-old mother of four, headed for work as a secretary in Cranbury, New Jersey. She was struggling not to cry when she noticed a man waving at her from a passing car.

She didn't pay much attention to him. But the next morning, the same car went by her. Again, the driver waved. Mary Ann looked a little closer and noticed he was good-looking. It soon became a daily ritual. He would wave and smile and she would smile back.

"Over the years, I'd wonder what he was like and where he went each day," Mary Ann recalled in *Woman's World* magazine. The ritual lasted for five years, but ended when Mary Ann took a new job that required taking a different route to work. She felt sad that she would miss the man in the green Chevelle.

But fate wouldn't let that happen. She stepped onto the elevator at her new company—and stared face to face with the stranger himself! She blurted out a hello but he was too stunned to respond.

"Don't you know who I am?" Mary Ann asked him.

Ray smiled shyly and replied, "Sure. But I almost didn't recognize you without a windshield."

After they introduced themselves, they discovered that, amazingly, they worked for the same company. The two quickly became close friends, but they kept their relationship platonic because both were married.

"All these years I'd wondered what it would be like to take Mary Ann in my arms," Ray recalled. "But it seemed like having her in my dreams would have to be enough."

They eventually confided in each other that they were unhappy in their marriages. Within a year, they each were divorced and began dating each other. A year later, the couple became engaged and were wed in 1978.

After sixteen happy years, Mary Ann told *Woman's World,* "From the first moment we saw each other, we were fated to be together."

❤ ❤ ❤

Helen and David Farrell-Garcia claim they found love while driving on the San Diego Freeway.

In 1992, Helen was motoring down the freeway when she and another driver began flirting with each other. "I looked over as this car was passing me to see this man mouthing the words, 'I love you,'" Helen recalled. "I smiled and he motioned for me to roll down my window."

While maintaining speeds of fifty-five miles an hour, they began chatting and when David asked for her phone number, she gave it to him. They went on a date and sparks flew. A year later, they were man and wife.

Love at First Byte

Lovebirds Mark Cooper and Teresa Burtick carried out a transatlantic long-distance romance completely by computer.

After months of "talking" to each other via modem, they fell terminally in love even though they had never met each other. In fact, Mark proposed to Teresa on his computer. And she typed her answer back: "Yes!!! I will."

The modem-day romance began when their computers connected through an international bulletin board in 1993. For the price of a local phone call, they were soon spending hours each night sending computer messages back and forth to each other—Teresa from her home in Indiana, Pennsylvania, and Mark from four thousand miles away in Howden, England.

"Within a few weeks, we were pretty good buddies," Teresa, twenty-seven, told reporters. "But after about six months I started to realize my feelings were deeper than that. I plucked up my courage and told Mark I thought I was falling in love with him."

Mark, twenty-three, an employee with a television listings company, was shocked at first. But he soon realized that he was in love with Teresa too. Three weeks later, Mark, using his tag "Mega Byte," typed out a marriage proposal to Teresa under her code name "Murfy Brown." She excitedly accepted.

About a month later, Mark hopped on a jet and flew to the United States to meet his computer bride-to-be.

"We spent two weeks together—and we loved each other just as much in person as over the computer," said Teresa. "He's the greatest guy. He's a real English gentleman. That was obvious by what he had to say on the screen—and even more so in person. Everybody thought I was crazy. But when I finally met Mark and he held me in his arms, I knew for sure he was the guy for me."

Mark admitted to reporters that some people might see this computer courtship as a bit odd. "But the advantage of a computer romance is that it lets you link up with the core of a person's personality," he said. "I feel I know Teresa every bit as well as if she had been the girl next door and not living across the Atlantic."

Radio Romance

Englishman Ken Stone was an avid CBer who used the handle "State Express." By chance—or what he believes was fate—Ken began chatting with a woman he knew only as "The Duchess." There was something about her voice and manner that intrigued him. He simply had to meet her.

Ken eventually discovered her true identity—and got the shock of his life.

In Exeter, England in 1991, "State Express" was talking on his CB when he became enthralled with "The Duchess." Of all the women he had heard on the air, none had affected him the way she had. It was all very innocent. "The Duchess" was just being friendly as most CBers are. But to Ken, she was special, and he wanted to know why.

"State Express" had to meet "The Duchess" in person, so he asked if they could get together.

"The Duchess" hesitated because she was not in the habit of inviting strangers over to her house. Yet she couldn't help but get a warm feeling whenever she heard his voice.

Totally out of character, "The Duchess" agreed to see "State Express." By CB, she directed him to her house.

When Ken arrived at her door, he was floored. "The Duchess" turned out to be Joyce Isaac, a former girlfriend he hadn't seen in twenty-three years. When Joyce realized who "State Express" was, she nearly fainted from surprise.

But it was Ken who received the bigger shock when his fifty-one-year-old ex-flame led him into the house where she introduced him to twenty-three-year-old Juliet—the daughter he never knew he had!

"We all fell into each other's arms laughing and crying," Ken, sixty, later told reporters.

Joyce recalled that she and Ken had an affair which he broke off. The last time they had seen each other, both were married to other people.

"He didn't have any idea he had made me pregnant," Joyce said. Although her marriage crumbled, she refused to tell Ken about his daughter because she didn't want to ruin his marriage. Joyce didn't know that he eventually got a divorce too.

She hadn't heard from Ken for more than two decades—until "State Express" asked over the CB to meet "The Duchess" in person. They began dating right away, wondering what fate had in store for them next.

7

Wrong Number, Right Woman

A wrong number turned into romance for two strangers living 750 miles apart.

Twice in one day in 1986, Scott Luczak of Columbus, Ohio, misdialed and reached Connie Powers of Andover, New Hampshire, by mistake. But both liked what they heard.

Scott, a thirty-four-year-old computer analyst at the time, had been trying to reach a New Hampshire company. But he dialed the wrong number and woke up Connie, an occupational therapist, who was sleeping late.

"I got you out of bed, didn't I?" Scott asked. He apologized and hung up.

Six hours later, he tried to call the company again. But he reached the same wrong number.

"This time we talked about half an hour," Scott recalled. "But like a fool, I forgot to ask for her last name and phone number. I didn't know what number I had dialed to reach her."

So Scott had to wait until his phone bill arrived a month later to find Connie's number printed on his long-distance charges. When he saw her number, he called Connie again—this time on purpose. They talked for about an hour and the next weekend they chatted again.

"The next call lasted two hours," said Connie, a divorced mother of one. "Then it was three hours, and four and five hours. There were even two six-hour phone calls. Each time we talked, we got to know each other better. We talked about everything—sports, childhoods, money, jobs, relationships, family values. I found myself looking forward more and more to his calls."

Three months after the first wrong call, Connie flew to Columbus. When they met for the first time, they gave each other a big hug. "It was almost like greeting an old friend," said Scott, who was also divorced. "I felt so comfortable being with her."

Shortly after Connie returned home, Scott took vacation time and drove sixteen hours in the snow to New Hampshire to spend Christmas with her. The first thing Scott did when he returned home to Ohio days later was call Connie and propose. "Naturally I said yes," recalled Connie. "Then I caught myself, thinking how ironic it was that even Scott's marriage proposal came over the phone."

After looking over their phone bills—about eight hundred dollars apiece during their courtship—Scott joked that it was cheaper to marry than to carry on a long-distance romance.

Scott quit his job and moved to New Hampshire. But their relationship hit hard times and they never got married. Eventually, Scott returned to Ohio.

"We're still friends," said Connie in 1995. "I'm glad we were in each other's lives. I think we stayed together longer than we should have because we kept thinking, 'There must be a reason why we were brought together.'"

The Swindle That Led to Love

Thanks to the lowest point in Richard Martin's life, he was able to experience his happiest moment.

In 1988, Richard, then a twenty-eight-year-old farm implement mechanic from Burrows, Indiana, was among the estimated thirty thousand lonely men swindled by the Church of Love. The church solicited cash and gifts in exchange for love letters from wayward young women the organization claimed it was "revirginizing." *People* magazine wrote about the scam and included a photo of a sad-faced Richard who had been fleeced out of five thousand dollars. "I live a cold, silent life," he told the magazine. "They [the church] gave me a feeling of security, that someone really cared about me."

The article spurred nineteen women to write Richard, offering him comfort. One of the women was Betsy Peelor, then twenty-two, of Bethel Park, Pennsylvania, who wrote:

Dear Richard,

Please forgive me if this comes across a bit strange. I read about you and I felt like I had to reach out to you . . . give you a hug or something. Just the few words that you spoke touched something inside of me, that if there was anything I could do to help, then I had to at least try. Maybe it's enough right now to know that someone is thinking about you and hoping you feel better about yourself.

Betsy's letter moved Richard to call her and they soon developed a relationship over the phone. Several months later, Betsy drove to Burrows for a visit. "I just started talking a mile a minute and we talked all night until it was morning," she recalled.

"I think it was good the way Richard and I met because we got to know each other without seeing each other."

After two visits, the couple had fallen in love. Betsy moved in with Richard and got a job as a cook at a senior citizen center in nearby Delphi. Six months later, in 1990, they got married.

In 1995, reflecting on their five-year marriage which has produced two children, Richard said, "Before Betsy came along, there wasn't anybody I ever wanted to marry. I was pretty down. But sometimes good things can come out of something bad. That's what happened to me."

Mr. and Mrs. Write

Pen pals into married mates? It can happen. Just ask Robert and Theresa George.

When Theresa was a single mother, she participated in Christmas '94 Operation Dear Abby in which the well-known columnist asked readers to write letters to lonely servicemen. Theresa penned a letter to Robert, an army sergeant stationed in Texas. The two hit it off right away and their back-and-forth correspondence soon advanced to long-distance calls.

"We spoke to each other on the telephone for three months," recalled Theresa in a letter to Abby published in her column. "It may sound preposterous, but we actually fell in love. We decided that we couldn't wait any longer to meet, so on February 17, 1995, I flew to Texas for a weekend. As soon as our eyes met, we knew we were right for each other.

"Robert and I were married an hour and a half after I stepped off that plane!

"Thank you from the bottom of our hearts. And my little 2-year-old daughter thanks you for her new daddy. We will be forever grateful to you for bringing us together."

Replied Abby, "My warmest congratulations. I wish you a long and fulfilling marriage."

❤ ❤ ❤

Back in 1982, Chris Rogers, a ten-year-old boy from Ohio, decided to write to a pen pal. Wanting to correspond with another boy, he picked out a name in a magazine's pen pal register—Lawrence Christensen.

What Chris didn't know was that the magazine had made a mistake. Lawrence was really Laurene Christensen, an eleven-year-old girl from North Dakota. She answered Chris's letter and although he now knew that his new pen pal was a girl, he wrote her a reply. And so began a long-distance friendship that grew deeper over the years.

By the time they were in high school, they felt they were more than just pen pals. And when they finally met, they fell in love—so much so that Chris moved to North Dakota to attend college with Laurene. And it was there where they agreed to tie the knot after eleven years as pen pals.

Born to Be Married

Carol Mansfield and Chip Stalter were destined to marry each other. After all, they were born on the same day—and even shared the same maternity room!

Both entered this world on October 21, 1959, at Pascack Valley Hospital in Westwood, New Jersey. Chip weighed in at eight pounds, four ounces, while Carol tipped the scales at a hefty ten pounds, ten ounces. The babies "met" each other in the first hours of their lives after they were brought to their respective mothers who occupied the same hospital room.

"I fell for Chip right away," recalled Carol jokingly. "His diapers were just as cute as could be."

After Chip and Carol were taken home from the hospital, their paths didn't cross until they were teenagers. Incredibly, although they grew up only two blocks from each other, Carol and Chip never knew each other as youngsters. They went to different schools and each had a different set of friends.

They became acquainted when they attended the same high school as sophomores. "I thought Chip seemed nice, but so were all the other sophomores," said Carol. But in their senior year, the two teens began dating each other. After comparing notes a few weeks later, they realized they had been together before as infants.

The couple went steady but then split up when they attended different colleges. However, they discovered that they missed each other too much, so Carol transferred to Trenton State College in New Jersey just to be with Chip. In 1983, at the age of twenty-four, they became engaged and married sixteen months later—twenty-five years after sharing a maternity room together.

Added Chip, "I guess you could say we started out as a case of love at first sight."

❤ ❤ ❤

In 1962, Dorothy Armstrong and Doris Reichenbach became friends in the maternity ward after Dorothy gave birth to a boy, Robert, and Doris gave birth to a girl, Christine.

Although they lived in different towns, the mothers kept in touch and visited each other once in a while. Their little tykes, Christine and Robert, were occasional playmates until they were seven years old.

Boy and girl met again by chance ten years later, but they were unaware that they had once played together. Not until they began dating did they discover their link to the past. They fell in love and at the age of twenty-five decided to tie the knot in South River, New Jersey.

Recalled Robert's mother, Dorothy, "In the hospital, Doris and I talked about the possibility of our babies marrying some day. It actually happened."

❤ ❤ ❤

Childhood brain surgery led to love for Cheryl Roth and Larry Wolkoff.

Cheryl and Larry were born with hydrocephalus—excessive fluid in the brain. It used to be a fatal condition until an operation to drain built-up fluid was developed in the 1950s. In 1964 when Cheryl was two and Larry was four, they had surgery at New York University Medical Center. Because the operation had to be repeated over the years, they met in the same hospital as teens. They began to keep in touch by phone and started dating in 1988. Two years later they wed and started raising a family in Basking Ridge, New Jersey.

Looking for His Special K

Marina Lorentzatos told her son Evan, a Houston businessman, that she had found Miss Right for him. There were only a few complications, though. Marina didn't know the young woman's name; she thought it started with a K. And, oh yes, there was one other thing: the girl of his dreams lived six thousand miles away in Greece.

But that didn't stop Evan from searching for Miss Right . . . and finding her . . . and marrying her.

In the summer of 1991, during a business trip to Greece, Evan, then twenty-six years old, met several young people at a nightclub on the Greek island of Cephalonia. Among the patrons he talked with was an attractive English tour representative. They exchanged pleasantries and went their separate ways.

He forgot her name. She didn't forget his. The following year, Evan's mother was in Greece when she bumped into the tour representative. When the young woman learned who Marina was, she asked about Evan.

After Marina returned home, she told Evan about the beautiful young woman who would be just perfect for him. Marina gave him a detailed description of Miss Right, but confessed that she didn't get her name; it was a strange one that started with a K.

On his next business trip to Greece, Evan made it his mission to find his special K. When he arrived in Cephalonia, he went to the office where Marina had last seen the young woman. He looked around and finally found a pretty English tour rep who looked familiar and matched the description his mother had given him. Not only that but she wore a name tag that said Kazia Powell. He had found her. "I think you're supposed to be the woman of my dreams," Evan blurted.

Kazia laughed. They hit it off right from the start and went out three straight nights. "I knew she was the one," Evan recalled. "On the third day, I asked her to marry me. She giggled and suggested that we wait."

Over the next two years, their love continued to grow.

"We were with each other all the time and we never argued," said Evan. "We knew we were meant to be together."

On Valentine's Day, 1995, the couple married in a nine-hundred-year-old church in Almondsbury, England. "We simply had to get married on Valentine's Day," said Kazia, "because it was the finishing touch to an amazing romance."

Lottery of Love

Lotto millionaires Jonell Walts and Tony Chernetsky won more than money. Thanks to their good fortune, they won each other's hearts.

In 1985, Jonell, a forty-one-year-old divorced mother from Evansville, Indiana, thought she was the luckiest woman in the world when she won $3.3 million in the Illinois lottery. The only thing missing in her life was a good man. There were plenty of men who wanted to squire her, but she shunned them because they were gold-diggers.

But the following year, she found her man, Tony—at an Illinois Lottery Millionaires reunion party. Tony, a Vietnam vet and electrician from Davenport, Iowa, was attending the affair because he had won $1.59 million in 1986. He too was having problems in his social life. His sudden wealth had brought him letters from women who were chasing him for his money. Fed up, Tony tossed the notes in the trash. He wondered if he would ever find a woman who loved him for who he was inside. And then he met Jonell.

"That guy upstairs knows how to make things happen," said Tony. "I paid my dues in Vietnam. Jonell worked hard and raised her son by herself. We got rewarded."

The couple fell head over heels in love and eloped to Las Vegas and built their dream house.

"I knew the minute I saw him that he was the one for me," recalled Jonell. "We must have been supposed to win the lottery. It was the only way we could have met.

"The odds of finding someone I could love as much as Tony make winning the lottery seem easy."

Taking the Plunge

Hilda Vogel fell for her man—literally.

In 1940, the twenty-three-year-old medical secretary was visiting her brother's sixth-floor photo studio in New York. While waiting for him to close up for the evening, she donned her winter coat and gloves and summoned the elevator.

The elevator door opened and Hilda stepped forward. Unfortunately, there was no elevator; only a black void. She dropped down the shaft to what seemed like certain death. But the quick-thinking woman, who was wearing her thickest gloves, managed to grab the elevator cable to break her fall. She slid down and landed hard, but she wasn't badly injured.

When the ambulance arrived, Dr. Nathan Serlin, twenty-nine, of City Hospital, expected to find a lifeless body. Instead, the victim was sitting on the stairs next to the elevator shaft.

"People hovered around," Nathan recalled. "She was mortified. Her hands were greasy and burned. But all I could see were those blue eyes, the brightest blue I'd ever seen. They shined so in that dark hallway."

It was a good thing the hallway was dark. It hid his embarrassment moments later. When Nathan bent down to examine Hilda's hands, his stiffly starched white uniform pants split right up the backside.

Two days after treating her, Nathan, being the good doctor that he was, telephoned his patient to see how she was doing. She was recovering

nicely. Then he asked if he might call on her later and she said yes. They began dating and soon took the plunge—into marriage, not an elevator shaft.

More than fifty years later, Nathan told the *New York Times,* "I still love that lady I met on those stairs."

The Star of Oprah's Audience

One state trooper found his true love when he spotted her in the audience of the *Oprah Winfrey Show.*

In 1991, Trooper Francisco Carrera was working the desk at the state police headquarters in Elgin, Illinois. During a break, Francisco was watching a nearby TV set that, by chance, was tuned to Oprah's show. As he looked at Oprah standing among the audience, he caught sight of a pretty woman over the host's left shoulder.

"I thought to myself, 'Now, that's an attractive woman,'" the trooper recalled.

That night, Francisco, thirty-five, stopped at a Wal-Mart in nearby Naperville—and spotted the same woman again! Figuring it was fate, the trooper went up to her and introduced himself. Then he told her he recognized her from Oprah's show, which was taped in Chicago.

The woman, Loren Richardson, thirty, was flabbergasted. "I told him, 'I can't believe you picked me out of that crowd.'"

A short time later, the two began dating. Two years later, Francisco decided to propose to his beloved at the very place where he first met Loren—Wal-Mart.

Francisco arranged with the store officials to use the public-address system. Then he got two of Loren's friends to phone her and ask her to meet them at the store.

After she arrived, she heard a familiar voice over the PA system saying, "Attention, Wal-Mart shoppers. Give me five minutes of your time and I'll tell you a story that will restore your faith in fate. I found my true love here after seeing her on the *Oprah Winfrey Show*."

Loren walked toward the service desk where Francisco was telling shoppers about her. When he spotted her in the crowd, he announced, "These people gave me some of their time. I want you to give me your life." Then he got down off the counter and said, "Loren, I love you. Will you marry me?" Loren tearfully and joyfully said yes as Francisco slipped an engagement ring on her finger.

Recalled Loren, "The way he proposed was the most romantic thing that ever happened to me. I was crying like a baby. Thank goodness for the *Oprah Winfrey Show*."

❤ ❤ ❤

Meeting by Accident

Christi Carter says it was an accident, but her husband Mark isn't so sure.

They began dating each other after Christi dumped a trayload of food in his lap at a restaurant where she worked.

"The first time I met her was at a bar in 1975," recalled Mark. "We talked a little bit and when she was getting ready to leave I told myself, 'Say something smart before she goes.' So I told her, 'I'm going to marry you some day.' She just laughed. But before she left, she wrote down her phone number on a matchbook cover and gave it to me. I called her several times, but no one ever answered. I figured she had given me a phony number so I threw the matchbook away."

The "accident" happened four months later. Mark, a twenty-three-year-old contractor at the time, stopped in for lunch at a restaurant called the Arctic Circle. Christi, then twenty-three, was a waitress there. She spotted Mark and went up to his table.

"She was holding a tray full of food and she said, 'I know you. I met you somewhere.' But I just couldn't remember her."

"She said something like, 'Nice memory. Great. I was the girl you were going to marry.'

"That's when she dropped the tray and everything on it went all over me—a large Coke, two cheeseburgers, and a couple of plates of fries."

Recalling the incident, Christi said, "It was an accident—I think. You know, how you talk with your hands."

Mark added, "And then it hit me. This was the girl who'd given me her phone number—the girl I wanted to marry."

They began dating, fell in love, and married. They now have two children and own a hotel, inn, and restaurant in Eureka, California. After sixteen years of marriage, Mark said, "It's funny how people end up meeting."

Popping the Question

Copping a Plea

Police Sgt. Jeffrey Fulcher had his girlfriend jailed—just so he could pop the question!

Jeffrey, then a thirty-five-year-old cop from Weehawken, New Jersey, had been dating Linda Antenucci, then 40, for three years. In 1991, he finally decided it was time to ask her to marry him. Rather than offer a traditional proposal, Jeffrey decided to make it an arresting moment.

He had another officer confront Linda with a bogus summons as she left a diner. The citation accused her of sending inflammatory letters to city officials. The officer then escorted a shocked Linda to the police station and put her in an unlocked cell.

Jeffrey soon entered and told Linda that it was a false arrest. Then he asked her to marry him. The still-stunned Linda responded with "Yes!"

But when she was released, she jokingly told her friends, "I am going to kill him!"

❤ ❤ ❤

One lovestruck man was so nervous about proposing to his girlfriend that he had a cop do it for him.

In 1992, Mark Webb was driving with his girlfriend, Wendy Coull, through Grants Pass, Oregon. Mark had an engagement ring in his pocket and was trying to get up the nerve to ask her to marry him.

Meanwhile, he was not paying attention to the speed limit and was nailed by Deputy Sheriff Michael O'Donnell for speeding. As the officer was about to issue a ticket, Mark took him aside and asked O'Donnell if he would surprise Wendy by giving her the ring.

The deputy agreed. He then asked Wendy to get out of the car, saying he had found something in Mark's pocket that had to do with her. Nervous and scared, Wendy did what she was told. She still wasn't sure what was happening when the deputy handed her the engagement ring. But she quickly broke into a smile when Mark got down on bended knee and proposed.

Wendy said yes.

As a wedding gift, O'Donnell let Mark off with a warning.

All in Favor

Michael McHone's marriage proposal to his future wife Nancy is a matter of public record in Nantucket, Massachusetts.

During their five-year courtship, Michael always told Nancy that when he proposed, the whole town would know at once. And he promised to do it in a way that had never been done before.

Nancy had forgotten about his pledge when they attended a town meeting in 1991. About 11 P.M. Michael stood up in the audience to speak. He said how wonderful it was that a North Carolina guy like him now felt Nantucket was his home. "Who'd ever think a southern gentleman like me would come here and have a New England girl steal my heart?"

Recalled Nancy, "I thought, 'Michael, this is not the place to be chatting with everyone.' It wasn't until he pulled a ring box from his pocket that it all started making sense."

Turning to the moderator, Michael said, "I don't know whether it's an amendment or a proposal." Then, looking in his girlfriend's startled eyes, he added, "But, Nancy, will you marry me?" He knelt in front of Nancy and held out a diamond engagement ring. Everyone applauded.

"In that moment, the five hundred people around me weren't there anymore," recalled Nancy. "It was just Michael and me. Tears of joy streamed down my face."

After watching the romantic scene unfold, the moderator told the crowd, "They'll never believe this at the Massachusetts Moderators Convention. All those who think Nancy should say yes, say 'aye.'" The townspeople roared their approval.

"If I had said no, it [her rejection] wouldn't have carried," recalled Nancy. "Being a reserved Yankee, I was embarrassed to have the whole town witness our intimate moment. But looking back, I'm glad Michael did it that way. As Michael says, our engagement will always be a matter of public record. And he can't wait to show the grandkids the minutes of that historic town meeting."

In a Class of Her Own

Tool salesman Craig Nelson had been dating grade school teacher Becky Klein for seven months when he decided to propose. In 1991 Nelson secretly visited Summit Hall Elementary School in Gaithersburg, Maryland, where he enlisted the cooperation of principal Lois Bell and Becky's students to assist him in pulling off his plan.

On the big day, the principal called Becky out of her sixth-grade class. Then Craig slipped into the classroom and asked the twenty-four students to help him spring a surprise on their teacher. The kids happily became accomplices.

"I had a bunch of foot-square papers, each inscribed with a letter in black magic marker ink," recalled Craig, who brought along a buddy to videotape the moment.

Handing each student one of the home-made flash cards, Craig lined them up in the back of the room and then sat down at Becky's desk. When she came in with the principal, Becky was shocked to see her boyfriend at the head of the class.

"Hello, sweetheart," Craig told her. "I was in the neighborhood and I thought I'd stop in. But your students have something to ask you."

On cue, the smiling boys and girls lifted the cards above their heads to spell out: BECKY, WILL YOU MARRY CRAIG? Craig then dropped to one knee and personally asked Becky to become his wife.

"I was flabbergasted," Becky recalled. "I dropped my books, burst into tears, hid my face in my hands and felt a lump in my throat the size of a Mack truck. Then from somewhere, I heard the word 'yes' stutter out."

The students and principal broke out in cheers and happy tears. Said student Brooke Bailey, "It was just like a fairy tale, just like a movie."

Love Me Tender

Businessman David Shaw gave new meaning to the words "tender offer."

In 1993, David placed an ad—in the style of a corporate bid—in the business section of the *Chicago Tribune,* announcing a tender offer by him for the affection of Christine Ott.

The ad read: "The purpose of this offer is to exchange love, loyalty and fidelity for an equal partnership in a new joint venture to be formed for the purpose of exploring the unchartered reaches of the future, to mine for the richness and reap the rewards believed to be contained therein."

Aware of the Securities and Exchange Commission's concerns about risky ventures, David, who was previously married, made sure the ad spelled out the speculative nature of the tender. "This offer may contain significant risk and is therefore suitable for a certain eligible investor only," it read.

David, fifty-three, president of Harbor Capital Corporation in suburban Chicago, also said in the ad that the "affection sought in this offer must be tendered in person."

Christine, thirty-one, an account group supervisor at Golin/Harris Communications, had been dating David for several years. She was unaware of the ad until she arrived at work where several excited colleagues pointed it out to her.

"I was surprised and a little embarrassed," Christine admitted later. "We're kind of private people. After I read the ad, I phoned David and told him I was considering his tender offer and was prepared to give him his answer that evening."

Over dinner, David proposed in person and Christine accepted. She found a token of his sincerity—a diamond ring—in her champagne glass.

David later told the *Wall Street Journal* he thought about including in the ad that he was being assisted in the transaction by "Hope, Less, Romantic & Associates." But, he reconsidered because, "I thought that it was too corny."

The Proposal Witnessed by Forty Million

TV sportscaster Ahmad Rashad knew he would be either crowing like a rooster or looking like a turkey when he made an on-the-air Thanksgiving Day proposal to *The Cosby Show* costar Phylicia Ayers-Allen.

At the time, Ahmad and Phylicia had been seeing each other quietly for several months. They began dating after the former football star asked his friend Bill Cosby to introduce him to Phylicia, who played Cosby's wife on the show. One night over dinner in 1985, Ahmad brought up the subject of marriage to Phylicia. "I asked Phylicia what she'd say if I asked her to marry me," Ahmad recalled. "Her answer was simple: 'I can't tell you what my answer would be because you haven't asked me.'"

A few days later, Ahmad was at the Silverdome in Detroit for NBC's nationwide televised coverage of the Thanksgiving Day game between the Lions and New York

Jets. Ahmad had asked producers for extra airtime during his live segment on the pregame show, "NFL '85," which they granted.

"I figured that if I really loved this lady I would have no problem proposing to her in front of all those people [an estimated forty million viewers] watching on TV," said Ahmad. He then surprised everyone by looking into the camera and announcing that he wanted Phylicia to be his wife.

"To this day I still don't know exactly what I said," Ahmad recalled. "But at the end I felt relieved, and I thought, 'Well, I did it. This girl could make me the most embarrassed man in America, but at least it's over now.'"

A surprised Bob Costas, host of the pregame show, joked on the air that he felt like Chuck Woolery, emcee of the *Love Connection.* Costas promised Ahmad that the intrepid "NFL '85" staff would bring Phylicia, who was in New York at the time, to their Rockefeller Centre studio so she could deliver her answer on the air at halftime.

"This is Thanksgiving Day," Ahmad said on the air. "If she doesn't accept my proposal, I'll be the biggest turkey in the nation."

Incredibly, when Phylicia finally appeared on camera, Ahmad did not hear or see her accept his proposal.

As the first half came to a close, Ahmad nervously gazed at a small TV monitor at the stadium so he could see what was happening in the studio back in New York. Recalled Ahmad, "I heard the director in my earpiece say, 'Ahmad, we've found Phylicia. We've got her right here. She's got an answer for you.' At that very moment, the monitor went blank.

"I could still hear them in the studio in New York, and I knew that my picture was on in most homes. Suddenly, the audio went dead too. Dick Enberg, the play-by-play man, was standing nearby. He was all wired up, connected to the studio. He was hunched over, listening. Then he started laughing.

"What if she said no? I wondered. But she had said yes. I was about the only person in the country who didn't know what she had said."

Phylicia recalled that she could barely talk. "Anytime something very great happens to me, I can't speak," she said. "I was so surprised, but it seemed so right that there was nothing to say but yes."

What if Phylicia had declined? "I would have told everybody to stay tuned because at the end of the show, I'm going to blow my brains out," said Ahmad.

When Ahmad returned home, his answering service was swamped with messages, including one from Bill Cosby, who complained that Ahmad had made life miserable for other husbands. Said the comedian: "My wife came downstairs and cracked me on the head, saying, 'Why didn't you propose to me like that?' I explained, 'I wasn't on TV then, dear.' She said, 'Well, you could have done *something!*'"

Sharing the Moment

Although most proposals are intimate, romantic moments when couples are alone, many other men like Ahmad Rashad find strength in numbers and pop the question in front of an audience.

Several times during a morning show in 1989 on WKGR in Fort Pierce, Florida, popular radio personality Dennis Heart told his thirty thousand listeners to stay tuned for an important announcement at 8:30 A.M.

When it was time, he played the theme from *Romeo and Juliet.* He announced that he had been involved with girlfriend Joann Mileni for a year and then said, "I thought I'd take this time to ask her to marry me."

He added that his first marriage was "for practice," but that this one would be "for life."

Knowing that Joann always tuned in to his show, Dennis asked her to call him back on the station's toll-free request line with her answer. The minutes ticked away, but Joann didn't answer her boyfriend's love plea.

However, three women named Joann called up and accepted Dennis's marriage proposal. So did two other women who claimed they would change their name to Joann.

When he still hadn't heard from the girl of his dreams, the now-nervous DJ jokingly proposed to Kevin Berry, the station's airborne traffic announcer.

Finally, nearly an hour later, Joann walked into the studio. She asked Dennis to get down on his knees and repeat his proposal. He did—and she said yes. They were married a week later.

❤ ❤ ❤

In 1991 at a K mart in Corvallis, Oregon, employee John Robinson got on the store's public address system and announced, "Attention K mart shoppers!" But the message that followed was aimed not at the customers, but at a fellow worker.

"Will Karen Means give me the honor of her hand in marriage?" John asked over the speaker. Then with roses and a ring, he hustled back to the toy department to look for Karen. When he found her, she threw her arms around him and gave him a big kiss. John took that to mean yes.

Customers in the aisle applauded as John helped his new fiancée put on her engagement ring.

❤ ❤ ❤

Rich Striler proposed to his girlfriend Carmen Verseman in "plane" sight.

Although they had been dating for some time, Rich had never mentioned marriage. But unknown to Carmen, Rich decided he wanted to tie the knot. So he secretly enlisted family members' help in his plan to snare her as his bride.

During a family reunion in 1992 in St. Libory, Illinois, Rich talked Carmen into going for a quick ride in her uncle's plane. Seconds after the plane took off, dozens of relatives rushed out onto the runway and positioned their bodies in such a way to spell out a message that could only be seen from the air.

With the plane airborne, Rich told his sweetie to look down. Carmen gazed out the window and gasped. Below her was a human message that spelled out WILL U MARRY ME. Carmen instantly turned to Rich and gushed, "Yes!"

❤ ❤ ❤

In the musical *Once Upon a Mattress,* Prince Dauntless asks Princess Winifred for her hand in marriage.

Life imitated art in 1991 during rehearsals in a Labette Community College production in Parsons, Kansas. Darren Helms, who played the prince, knelt in front of Lorraine Hobson, who portrayed the princess, and asked her to marry him—for real.

"She realized what was happening," recalled director Kenton Kersting. "The entire company around them realized what was happening, and they all cheered and clapped when she said, 'Sure.'"

Thumbs up for Engaging Stories

Romantics have turned to the silver screen at local theaters to propose.

In 1990, Kevin O'Keefe, twenty-five, a salesman from Saddle River, New Jersey, made a four-minute movie to woo girlfriend Beth Corey, twenty-five, into marriage.

"I'm the kind of guy who always wants to do things differently," Kevin recalled. "I wanted to come up with a way to propose that was so unique that fifty years from now—when I'm bald and weigh four hundred pounds—Beth can still look back and cherish the moment when I asked her to be my wife."

Because he worked in a film company, Kevin decided to make his own low-budget movie. He cast three hairy buddies who dressed up as women—complete with padding, heavy lipstick, rouge, and blue wigs.

"They were the ugliest bunch of 'females' I'd ever seen," he said. "Their five o'clock shadow was showing and their legs and arms were covered with hair. It wasn't a pretty sight."

In the movie, the "ladies" are seated at a table when Kevin comes in. They all make plays for him, but he keeps saying, "No, no, no!" Another man comes in with a photo of Beth. Kevin looks at it and says, "I'll take her if she'll have me." Then he turns to the camera, pops the question and produces a ring—and the film ends.

Kevin persuaded a local theater to let him show his flick—which cost about one thousand dollars to produce—before the coming attractions and the feature film. Then he secretly invited friends and family members to be part of the audience. He told his unsuspecting girlfriend that he was taking her to see *Pretty Woman*.

"We sat down, the theater went dark and this weird silent movie with subtitles came on," recalled Beth, a teacher in Hackensack. "I thought, 'This can't be *Pretty Woman*.' Then it slowly began to sink in that I was watching a film starring Kevin and his friends. And in the last few seconds he was proposing marriage to me. I didn't know whether to laugh or cry or faint. Finally, I managed to say 'yes.'

"Then the lights came on in the theater, and everyone was cheering and clapping for us. I saw my family and friends scattered all over the theater. It was the happiest day of my life—and something I'll never forget as long as I live."

❤ ❤ ❤

In 1992, Carin Russo went on a date with her beau Bob Stevens in the Buffalo suburb of Cheektowaga expecting to see *The Bodyguard*. Unknown to Carin, twenty-three, Bob had purchased four hundred dollars' worth of space with Screen Seen, a company that markets advertising slides projected on the screen between films.

Bob, twenty-six, arranged for three slides to be shown. The first was a picture of Carin as a child with the question, "Does anyone in the theater know this person?" While Carin threw her hands up to her face in surprise, the next slide said, "The person next to you has an important question to ask you."

Bob then jumped to his feet and waited for the final slide to appear—a picture of the couple. He then asked Carin to be his bride. Teary-eyed, Carin said yes and Bob slipped an engagement ring on her finger.

The theater lights went up, and the audience stood and cheered the couple who were congratulated by about fifty relatives and friends who had entered the theater unseen by Carin. "I was in shock," recalled Carin.

❤ ❤ ❤

Joe Pugh, twenty-one, of Nashville tried a similar approach to win the heart of his love, Karen Williams, twenty.

He took her to the movies after alerting about forty friends and family of his secret plan. They went inside the theater without Karen noticing.

As the couple watched the coming attractions, Karen stared in disbelief as a slide appeared on the screen showing Joe down on one knee with his hand over his heart.

"Joe," Karen stammered. "That's you!"

In the next slide on the movie screen, Joe was seen holding a sign that read KAREN. It was followed by a final slide of Joe holding another sign over his head that read, WILL YOU MARRY ME?

Recalled Joe, "It took Karen five minutes to recover enough to say yes." When he announced her answer to the audience, their friends and family stood up and cheered.

"Joe really caught me off guard with his proposal," admitted Karen. "Once the movie finally started, I went to the bathroom about five times to wipe away the tears."

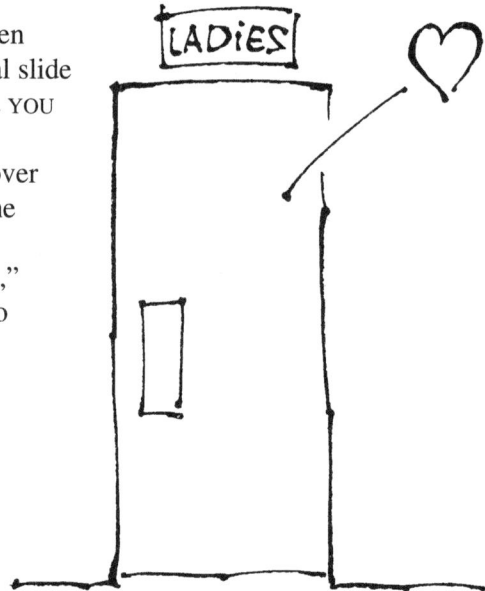

Puzzling Proposals

Crossword clues have led couples to matrimony.

When Jean Sherman fell in love with Peter Chatzky in 1988, she wanted a creative way to propose to him. Since the Manhattan couple were both enthusiasts of the crossword puzzles in the *New York Times,* she was struck with an idea.

Jean wrote to puzzle editor Eugene Maleska and asked if he would let her make a marriage proposal in a *Times* crossword. He wrote back, "I can disguise it in a June, 1989, daily puzzle. The entries would include JEAN PROPOSES MARRIAGE and THOU ART PETER, a quotation from Matthew 16:18. I'm sending a copy of your letter to one of my best constructors."

In the letter he added, "Incidentally, my first puzzle was a personal one, created for a beautiful coed in the same college that I attended. Her name was Jean, and I knew she liked crosswords. I sent her a puzzle. JEAN was 1 Across. The clue was 'Most beautiful girl on campus.' Later we married and had forty-three happy years together until cancer took her away from me in 1983. May you and Peter have the same joy for many years to come. Pax, amor et felicitas."

After some miscommunication with his constructor, Maleska told Jean that the special puzzle would run on September 11, 1989.

Early that morning, Jean got the *Times* and urged Peter to do the crossword. She recalled that he went pale when he began deciphering the key clues: 1 Across, "Actress Arthur or Simmons"; 5 Across, "Matthew 16:18"; 49 Across, "Tank or Civil War general"; 10 Down, "Declares intention to wed"; 39 Down, "Love and _____, 1955 Emmy-award song"; and 36 Down, "Wedding ceremony response."

"I put the paper down, and said, 'Uh, I don't think I'm ready to do this puzzle,'" Peter recalled. But two years later Peter and Jean were married. They framed the crossword puzzle and hung it over their bed.

❤ ❤ ❤

In 1991, Stanford University law student Neil Nathanson asked *San Francisco Examiner* crossword puzzle creator Merl Reagle to create a personal puzzle that Neil, thirty-one, could give his girlfriend, Leslie Hamilton, twenty-four, as his marriage proposal.

Reagle declined—and instead suggested that he and Neil create a full-fledged crossword that would appear in a Sunday issue of the newspaper. For the next four months, Neil provided personal tidbits about his lady love which Reagle incorporated into clues.

When the crossword appeared in the newspaper's *Image* magazine, Leslie was amazed that some of the answers fit her profile: Her birth place, MONTANA ("State or quarterback"); her favorite instrument, CELLO ("Sit-down string"); her favorite pet, DACHSHUND ("Adorable dog"); her first name, ("Actress Caron") and her boyfriend's ("Astronaut Armstrong").

"I just chalked it up to coincidence," Leslie recalled. But there was no way she could ignore the message that she solved in the special red squares at the center of the puzzle: DEAR LESLIE WILL YOU MARRY ME—NEIL.

Leslie responded with a three-letter word for affirmative and a four-letter word for lip-lock.

Cheeky Honey Mooner

Many romantic men have used billboards and scoreboards to ask for their sweetheart's hand in marriage. But then there are guys like Paul Armstrong.

His girlfriend Connie Norman got the surprise of her life in 1995 when Paul asked her to give him a full body massage.

When she agreed, he took off his clothes and lay on his stomach. Tattooed on his rear end was the message "Connie, will you marry me?"

After she screamed with happiness, Connie responded by promising to have the word "yes" etched on her own posterior.

"I don't know what I'd have done if she'd given me the bum's rush," Paul told reporters in London where the couple live. "Connie hates tattoos. Luckily, it all worked out and now she says she even likes it."

Said Connie, "How could I say no after all that?"

❤ ❤ ❤

In 1990, when Bill Kenny, forty-three, of River Forest, Illinois, was ready to settle down, he wanted to do something memorable for his marriage proposal. So he arranged to take his love, Angela Martino, twenty-eight, to church and out for breakfast while a thirty-five-foot-tall balloon gorilla was inflated in the front yard of her home. Attached to the giant ape was a sign that read, STOP MONKEYING AROUND. MARRY ME.

Angela didn't suspect a thing until Bill drove her home. She took one look at the King Kong Cupid and announced she'd love to marry Bill. "I was stunned," she recalled. "Of course, I said yes. How could I resist?"

❤ ❤ ❤

In 1992, Michael Kase, a film production assistant on the set of the TV soap opera *The Bold and the Beautiful,* used a cue card to say what was in his heart.

His intended, actress Schae Harrison, who played Darla on the show, was expecting to do a scene in which she answers the door and receives a telegram. Instead, when she opened the door, she found Michael holding a cue card off camera with the question, WILL YOU MARRY ME?

Recalled Schae, "I was in shock. I hyperventilated and I said, 'Oh my God!' about twenty-nine times. Then I threw my arms around him and said, 'Yes.'"

Moonstruck

When Don Pifalo proposed to sweetheart Irene Kocsis, he promised her the moon—and meant it.

He drew up a deed giving her ownership of the moon and then filed the document in the Hillsborough County Courthouse in Tampa, Florida, in 1991. The deed gave Irene the property in "consideration of love and affection." It appeared legal because the clerk's office recorded the deed without catching the reference to the moon.

"I can't give you any more than the moon," the fifty-five-year-old romantic said when he proposed to Irene, fifty-three.

She readily accepted the proposal from the real estate consultant. "What woman wouldn't want the moon?" Irene asked. "He's everything a woman could want. I'm lucky to have him."

Irene may have a hard time claiming the moon for herself, however. More than ninety nations signed a treaty in 1967 declaring "that neither the moon nor any other natural body in outer space may be claimed by any country or used for military purposes."

True Love

A Perfect Match

Randall Curlee won Victoria Ingram's heart—and one of her kidneys too.

For a wedding present, the bride donated her organ to the once-dying groom.

"I got the best gift I could ever have—the gift of life," declared Randall. "Without my wife's kidney, I would have died."

Victoria, a divorced real estate agent, met her future husband while he was house-hunting in 1992 in Mission Viejo, California. She was hosting an open house when Randall, an audio company executive in the midst of a divorce, walked in.

After they began dating, Victoria learned of Randall's daunting health problems. He had battled diabetes since childhood and sometimes suffered from insulin shock. In 1985, he was stricken by a heart attack and underwent a triple bypass operation. He also had laser surgery to restore the sight in his left eye which had been blinded by diabetes.

But she stuck by him and they planned to get married. However, Randall received another devastating health blow when the doctors told him that his kidneys were failing him. Without a transplant, he would be dead within a year.

Randall became one of twenty-seven thousand Americans who are candidates for the eight thousand donor kidneys available each year. Relatives volunteered to donate a kidney, but none proved to be a suitable match. Meanwhile, Randall's health slowly but steadily deteriorated. He gave Victoria a chance to back out of their engagement. Instead, she asked doctors to test her to see if she could give one of her kidneys to the man she loved.

Although the odds for compatibility were ten thousand to one, Victoria's kidney proved to be just what the doctor ordered. "The doctors were stunned to find she was a perfect match," Randall recalled.

To publicize the need for organ donations, Randall, forty-six, and Victoria, forty-five, allowed *Good Morning America* to broadcast their 1994 wedding live. The ceremony was held in the chapel of Sharp Memorial Hospital in San Diego.

A month later, the newlyweds underwent the four-hour, life-saving operation at the same hospital. The Curlees lay in separate rooms, each with its own surgical team. Victoria's kidney was removed, flushed clean and implanted into her groom. Although both faced risks from infection, blood loss and, in Randall's case, rejection, the couple sailed through the operation.

"She was so optimistic and persistent that she changed attitudes in the hospital," said Randall. "Before, the doctors were so cautious, trying to present the negative side of things. Victoria won everyone over."

A week after the surgery, the couple were taking a stroll when Victoria told reporters, "I'd do it again in a second. I hope for a better quality of life for my husband. He is my best friend. Wouldn't you want to have your best friend in the best of health?"

"Now we are united as never before."

For Love or Money

Morton Smith had an intriguing dilemma. He was in love with a woman of whom his mother disapproved. If he married her, he risked losing an inheritance of up to $100 million.

Morton picked love over money. Despite threats from his mother, superwealthy heiress Joan Irvine Smith, that she would disown him, Morton went ahead and wed his college sweetheart, Marianne Campbell, in 1994.

"I don't think anybody should have to be forced to choose between individuals and their family," Morton told reporters after the wedding. "I did the right thing as far as my heart told me."

Morton and Marianne met when both were undergraduates at the University of Rhode Island. The seventh of nine children, she grew up in Wilmington, a working-class suburb of Boston. After graduation, Marianne earned a master's degree in clinical psychology. She then became a pediatric oncology nurse at Long Beach (California) Memorial Medical Center. Meanwhile, Morton started a career as a securities broker in nearby Los Alamitos.

Marianne claimed that her relationship with her mother-in-law was rocky long before she got married. The day after the two women first met in 1987, Joan Irvine Smith took her on a shopping spree that Marianne likened to the great makeover in the film *Pretty Woman.*

"She didn't like the way I dressed," said Marianne. "She was determined to get me a whole new wardrobe."

47

Over the years, said Morton, family members told him that Marianne was not suitable for him to marry. He said that when word reached the family that he had proposed to Marianne, he was no longer welcome at home.

Morton claimed that his mother spent four hours one night ordering him to change his mind. "When I wouldn't, she said, 'I'm writing you out of my will. You've made your choice—now you're severed from your family forever. If you have children, they will never meet me.' Soon after, I got letters from my mother's lawyers telling me that I'd been written out of her will."

Marianne pressured Morton to cancel a planned wedding in May 1994, because she didn't want to compete with $100 million, Morton recalled. But a few months later, he proposed again. "I told Marianne, 'I love you with all my heart and I want to marry you. If you want to marry me, here's your chance.'"

She said yes and they wed in September in a small church with only sixty guests. Conspicuously absent were Morton's parents and two half-brothers.

A few weeks after the wedding, Joan Irvine Smith—who's worth an estimated $600 million—told the *Los Angeles Times* that the marriage "will be a continuing cause of estrangement from the rest of the family."

She added, "I am not in favor of any marriage for him right now, particularly not this marriage." She claimed that Marianne "was very antagonistic toward my relationship with my son" and that she was generally ungrateful.

Marianne told the *Times* that she was most saddened by the broken relationships. "It's a shame because they have a wonderful family, an incredible legacy," she said. "Mrs. Smith is brilliant. I just wish she could be more of a mom to him. I think sometimes she tries to control people. She can't control me because I can't be bought. I won't be. I don't want any bit of their inheritance. I have my own life. To deny your son—I can't think of anything more tragic than that."

Morton contended that he and Marianne would survive without the big money. "People call me insane, but I'd do it all over again because I love her with all my heart," he declared. "She's worth more than all the money in the world to me."

Even after 'Death Do Us Part'

Sometimes love is so strong that not even death can stop a couple from getting married.

In 1991 Nicola Ninivaggi, of Canelli, Italy, married his fiancée Giovanna Barbero—three days after she was murdered!

The heartwrenching service took place in the parish church at the day and place where the couple had planned to exchange their marriage vows. Tragically, just three days before the wedding, the twenty-five-year-old bride-to-be was stabbed to death after leaving a disco.

Even though Giovanna was dead, the devastated Nicola insisted that he marry the love of his life. "Nicola wanted her to enter heaven as his wife," Father Angelo Lumi explained to the Italian press. "It was an act of love."

The bizarre wedding ceremony was held moments before the funeral. Giovanna, dressed in her white wedding gown, was laid out in her coffin. The thirty-three-year-old groom stood over the open casket as teary-eyed friends and relatives gathered round.

Nicola gently placed a wedding ring on the finger of his lifeless bride. Although the ceremony wasn't sanctioned by the church, Father Lumi blessed the union and then conducted a funeral service for Giovanna.

Said Nicola, "It was a last way to tell Giovanna how much I loved her."

❤ ❤ ❤

In two separate cases in France, President François Mitterrand gave special permission for women to marry their deceased fiancés.

Anne-Marie Bernicot, thirty-five, had been all set to marry Pierre-Jean Camon in 1989. But just ten days before their scheduled wedding, the groom-to-be died of cancer.

Anne-Marie was heartbroken but she vowed that death would not cheat her out of marrying the man she loved. When she learned the law wouldn't let her wed a dead man, she appealed to Mitterrand. Although posthumous weddings are rare and normally given only in wartime when a woman is pregnant, the president granted her wish.

Nearly a year after Pierre-Jean died, Anne-Marie stood before the mayor of Cricqueboeuf, France. She wore a black and white dress—white for the bride she was, black for the widow she'd immediately become. Then, as family and friends watched, Anne-Marie recited the vows and was finally wed to the true love of her life.

Three years earlier, twenty-eight-year-old Corinne Tarride married her fiancé, Police Lieutenant François Klein, after he had been shot while trying to apprehend a gang of robbers. "People might think it's stupid and morbid, but to me it was recognition of the love we had," Corinne explained.

When François was buried with full police honors, Corinne decided she wanted to marry him anyway. "I was determined that those evil criminals who murdered the man I was to marry would not deprive me of my rights as a woman in love," she declared. "They shattered my dreams, but there was no way they were going to kill my memories, too. I wanted François and me to be man and wife forever—even though he was no longer on earth."

Ten months after she appealed to President Mitterrand, she was given permission to marry François. The 1986 ceremony at city hall in Ytrac, France, lasted about three minutes. She said the normal wedding vows and then placed the ring on her finger. "My husband may be dead," said Corinne, "but at least I'll carry his name and our love forever."

"*. . . in sickness and in health*"

Anthony Wenzel wasn't going to let a ruptured appendix prevent him from marrying his sweetheart, Christy Campbell.

Three days before their March 1994 wedding in Roanoke, Virginia, Anthony became feverish with pains in his stomach. "He thought he had a bad case of the flu," Christy recalled. "I thought he had had too much fun at his bachelor party in Atlantic City."

As his condition worsened, Anthony, an electrical engineer from Charlottesville, went to Martha Jefferson Hospital where doctors diagnosed the ruptured appendix.

"We need to get you in for surgery immediately," the surgeon said.

"I can't," Anthony replied. "I'm getting married in three days."

"You don't understand. You could die."

Recalled Christy, "I was in Roanoke two hours away getting ready for the wedding when I checked my voice mail. Anthony had called and said, 'By the time you get this message I'll be in surgery.'"

She rushed to the hospital and was by his side after the operation. Doctors had doubts that Anthony could make the wedding, but he was determined to wed Christy. "All those people were coming to the wedding, so I figured I better show up," said Anthony.

"We had contingency plans," said Christy. "Plan A: He walks down the aisle. Plan B: He is brought in on a wheelchair. Plan C: He is wheeled in on a gurney. Plan D: He can't get out of bed so I'll go to the hospital and marry him there."

Unfortunately, complications set in for Anthony. He had developed an infection. The night before the wedding, he was bedridden and feeling worse than ever—but still insisting he would make it to the ceremony.

"He couldn't be at the rehearsal dinner, which he and his family had spent a long time planning," said Christy. "I was there at a table with a cellular phone talking to him and describing things to him. We were both crying. He said it was the loneliest he ever felt."

On their wedding day, Christy got ready, not knowing for sure if the groom would show up. Meanwhile, Anthony convinced doctors to release him for a few hours so he could get married. They agreed only on the condition that he remain under the care of a physician in Roanoke who was a friend of Christy's family. Despite the pain and a distended stomach, Anthony got out of bed and into a waiting limo for the two-hour trip to Roanoke.

"I was pretty exhausted by the time we reached Roanoke," Anthony recalled. "I stayed in a hotel until about twenty minutes before the wedding. I had my doubts that I could make it to the church, but I knew I just had to be there."

More than three hundred people—including his grandmother and aunt and uncle who flew in from Germany—filled the First Christian Church. Not until the bride arrived and asked her father, "Is he here yet?" did she know for sure that Anthony had indeed shown up for the ceremony.

"It was a good thing I had two best men," said Anthony. "They pretty much carried me into the church. When Christy came down the aisle and we held hands, she whispered to me, 'I'm glad to see you made it.'"

Despite his weakened condition and pain, the groom held up long enough for the couple to get married and spend a little time together at the reception. "He couldn't eat or drink anything at the reception," she said. "But we still managed to celebrate our wedding—and his survival. We stayed for a few pictures and then we had to go." But instead of going on their planned honeymoon in Barbados, they spent it at Roanoke Memorial Hospital where Anthony was taken shortly after the wedding—in their limo.

Anthony soon underwent a five-and-a-half-hour operation that required a two-week recuperation. "We were put in the hospital's Presidential Suite which they renamed the 'Honeymoon Suite,'" recalled Christy, who stayed at the hospital with her new husband. (They finally went on their Caribbean honeymoon eight months later.)

"It's been an ordeal," she said from their home in Ruckersville, Virginia. "It makes you think about what's important—making sure you're healthy and you're there for each other.

"We found we had a lot of inner strength. In any marriage there are good times and bad times. We underwent the ultimate test right at the start—and we passed."

Prisoners of Love

Joann Russo and Phillip Labiano met, courted, and got married—all while locked away in jail!

It happened in 1987 at the Yavapai County Jail in Prescott, Arizona. The two first caught a glimpse of each other in a jailhouse hallway as guards were escorting them to and from their lawyers. Joann had been convicted of forgery and Phillip of trafficking in stolen goods. They were waiting to be sentenced.

"The second I saw her, I knew we belonged together," he told a reporter at the time. "I couldn't take my eyes off of her. My first thought was, 'What a beautiful woman. I could die happy if I could hold her in my arms for one moment.'"

The feeling was mutual. According to a news account, she said, "Phillip took my breath away. I wanted to reach out and put my arms around him. But we were surrounded by guards who wouldn't let us near each other."

As guards hustled them away in opposite directions, Phillip yelled to Joann that he'd see her again. A short while after he was returned to a high security isolation cell, he heard a woman's voice coming from the sink's plumbing. It was Joann's voice.

Day after day, they yelled their dreams, fears, and feelings through the jail plumbing. Then a week after their first meeting, they had another chance encounter. Joann was leaving her lawyer while Phillip was going to his. Defying the guards, the two stopped and held hands without saying a word.

Later, when Phillip was placed in a regular cell, he and Joann continued their courtship by shouting across a ten-foot passageway separating the men's and women's sections. By now, they had fallen for each other and began smuggling love letters through an accomplice.

Authorities caught them and threatened to throw both of them into isolation cells if they didn't stop trying to communicate with each other. But a month after they had first met, Phillip managed to send a letter to Joann asking her to marry him. She said yes.

Six weeks later, they received permission from a judge to get married. The couple exchanged vows—and paper rings—in the jail's exercise yard. After they were pronounced man and wife, they were allowed to kiss before guards separated them.

The next day, Joann was transferred to a state prison where she served six years. Phillip was sent to a different prison where he served eight years. According to Arizona Department of Corrections records, Joann was released in 1993 and went to Connecticut. Phillip was released in 1995—into the hands of California authorities, to answer an outstanding warrant.

No One Told the Groom He's Getting Married

Lynn Gerla and Mike Briggs, from Boise, Idaho, became engaged on Easter 1993, and planned a wedding for June 18, 1994. But in January they realized they didn't have enough money to pay for the wedding, so they decided to wait until they could afford to get married.

But then in March, Lynn was struck with a wonderful idea. Even if she couldn't have the elegant wedding she had always dreamed about, she could have one so special no one would ever forget it—especially the groom. She would throw a surprise wedding.

Without a word to Mike, Lynn arranged to hold the ceremony in her aunt's backyard gazebo on June 18—the original date of their wedding. She hand-delivered one hundred invitations to the guests, making them promise not to say a word to Mike. To make sure Mike would show up for the wedding, Lynn enlisted the help of her cousin Jeremy. He asked Mike to be a groomsman at his "wedding." Mike agreed.

While Lynn, twenty, an office manager, was secretly handling the arrangements, Mike, twenty-three, a personal fitness trainer, was wondering why they couldn't just get married.

"About three times a week, Mike would ask me to marry him," Lynn recalled. "He said we could elope or at least have a small wedding. I told him, 'When I'm ready, I'll let you know.' I felt badly for him, but I knew this was definitely how I wanted it to be."

Incredibly, despite all the running around that Lynn did to prepare for the wedding, and all the people who knew about the surprise, the secret remained intact.

When the big day arrived, Mike put on his tuxedo and stood by the gazebo, expecting to see Jeremy get married.

"Suddenly, I heard the song, *Pretty Woman,*" Mike recalled. "That's our song and I wondered what was going on. Then my mother stood up and pinned a boutonniere on me and said, 'I love you.'

"I was in awe, in shock. I kept telling myself, 'No way, this isn't really happening.' I mean, I had no clue. My mind was a blank when the groomsmen, who were originally going to be at our wedding, came out. I couldn't believe it. Then I saw Lynn in a wedding dress. She was walking down the aisle between my dad and her dad and she had a big grin."

Lynn walked up to the stunned groom and got down on her knee and asked, "Will you marry me?" In a booming voice, Mike replied, "Yes!" The guests clapped and the surprise wedding went off without a hitch.

"I loved it," recalled Mike. "I had no stress and didn't have to worry about the wedding plans. I'll remember that day for the rest of my life."

He admitted there was only one problem. "I'll never be able to top this surprise."

Seeing Is Believing

Blind couple Simon Stain and Wendy Jackson of Derby, England, fell in love and moved in together. But then Simon's vision miraculously returned, and he finally saw what his girlfriend looked like.

For Simon, it was love at first sight.

Simon's vision had been poor as a child. By the time he was a teenager, he suffered from night blindness and could see things in the daylight only if he held them in front of his eyes. By July 1990, Simon went totally blind and needed a guide dog to get around.

A few months later, Simon went to a job interview where he met Wendy. Although they were sightless, they could see they were meant for each other. They fell in love and moved in together.

And then one day Simon had the most amazing experience of his life—without warning, he regained his sight.

"I woke up one morning with the curtains shut and I could see the dim blue light of the sun shining through the blue material," he told reporters. "I remember asking myself if this was a dream. Then I saw Wendy. My sight was clearer than it had ever been. And she was so beautiful I had to tell her."

At first, Wendy confessed, she was worried that Simon would leave her because he had regained his sight. But he put her fears to rest by telling her he had fallen in love with her all over again. And then he asked her to marry him.

"I know Wendy had doubts that I would stay with her once I got my sight back," he said. "But I will always be there for her."

Odd Couples

Lotsa Love

In one of the most bizarre romances of the century, a teenage girl became engaged to a man who was nearly three times her age—and eight times her weight.

For five years, five-foot, 125-pound Tammy Humphreys lived with her six-foot, two-inch fiancé, Sylvanus "Hambone" Smith, who crushed the scales at nearly 1,000 pounds.

"People are astonished when they hear about us," Tammy admitted to a reporter in 1993. "But I love him. To me, he's a big gentle bear of a man."

Said Hambone, "She's a miracle from God. In my wildest dreams, I never thought I'd ever have such a wonderful woman as Tammy."

Tragically, before the couple got married, Hambone died in 1995 from heart failure.

Hambone had been huge his entire life. He weighed a whopping $15\frac{1}{2}$ pounds at birth. By the time he was eleven years old, he had grown to 275 pounds. The giant, who got his colorful nickname when he was seen gnawing on a ham bone, kept gaining weight. By the time he met Tammy, he sported a 103-inch waist, 70-inch thighs, and a 24-inch neck.

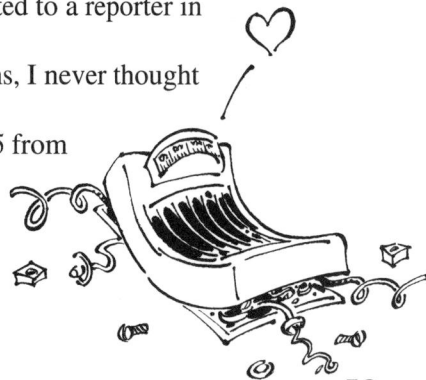

He was so large he couldn't even walk. He spent his days in bed at his home in Tifton, Georgia, where he ran a pawn shop. By that time, the divorced ex-chef had five grown children—who each averaged over 400 pounds.

Tammy first met Hambone in 1988 when she was sixteen and he was forty-seven. "I got very lonely lying here day after day," Hambone recalled. "Then one day Tammy came by with my youngest daughter Melissa. Tammy was having some problems in school, and I started giving her advice."

"He was the first man who ever listened to me," said Tammy. "I've had boyfriends before, but I've never been able to talk to anyone like I talked to him. We got closer until eventually we just fell in love."

Over the objections of her mother, Tammy moved in with Hambone when she was seventeen. "The way I look at it, we've all got faults," she said during their engagement. "Okay, he's big—so what? I'm not perfect either. As long as he can deal with me, I can deal with him."

Tammy and Hambone stayed together until his death.

❤ ❤ ❤

Friends good-naturedly have called Keith and Hazel Burton "Laurel and Hardy"—because at one point in the couple's marriage, Hazel weighed 650 pounds and Keith tipped the scales at a mere 147 pounds.

Hazel developed a crush on Keith in 1981 when they started chatting on CB radios in their hometown of Scunthorpe, England. "She had an incredibly sexy voice, a great sense of humor, and a fantastic personality," recalled Keith.

When they met for the first time at a CB rally, Keith was shocked by her size. "But it didn't take long for me to see further than her body," he said. "She still had the same bubbly personality I'd fallen in love with over the CB. It was just wrapped in a larger package than I expected."

Just three weeks after they met, the couple got married. The bride weighed more than twice the groom—her 325 pounds to his 140 pounds. The arrangements were made in such a rush that when the marriage license bureau clerk asked Hazel for Keith's last name, Hazel didn't even know it!

The Burtons have been happily married ever since. By 1993, the couple had five children, ranging in age from two and a half to eleven. But with each of her children's birth, Hazel packed on the pounds until she had doubled her wedding day weight and was now 650 pounds. Meanwhile, her husband had gained only seven pounds. Hazel finally went on a diet in an effort to match her weight as a bride—325 pounds.

"I love my husband and kids too much to eat myself to death," said Hazel.

The Long and the Short of Marriage

Love has a way of evening things out, according to Reginald Ilott and his wife Odette. He stands six feet, two inches; she's only three feet, eleven inches.

Yet they're a happily married couple with two children.

They have a boy with the same condition as his mother—a form of dwarfism—and a daughter who is expected to be tall like her father.

Reginald was nineteen and Odette twenty-one when they met in a bar in their hometown of Adelaide, Australia, in 1982. Despite the height differential, they were attracted to each other and eventually got married. But many people thought the couple didn't belong together. During their courtship and the first few years of their marriage, Reginald and Odette were forced to endure cruel comments from strangers.

"Only rarely now do we get stared at," Odette told reporters. "People seem to draw inspiration from seeing how loving we are to each other.

"We were out at a mall once and a little child said, 'Look at the funny lady. She's tiny.' That would have crushed Reg and me a few years ago, but all we did was smile and squeeze each other's hand tighter.

"The child's mother said, 'But look, sweetie, how big her smile is. And see what a happy family they are. That's a family with a lot of love.'"

❤ ❤ ❤

In 1980 in San Bernardino, California, six-foot, six-inch Delbert Gleason married three-foot, eight-inch Edwina Gleason after they were introduced on a blind date.

According to an article written shortly after their wedding, the Gleasons first met as high school students in 1975 when Delbert accidentally knocked over little Edwina as he ran for the bus. They didn't meet again until 1980 when they were invited on a blind dinner date by mutual friends.

"I looked up and thought, 'Oh, my God!'" Edwina recalled. "He was a little taller than I expected."

The date led to romance and then marriage. "I thought about the difference in size at first," admitted Delbert. "But she's more of a woman than a lot I've known. Height makes no difference."

And They Said It Wouldn't Last

In one of the most incredible May-December marriages ever, eighty-five-year-old Pia Curioni wed nineteen-year-old Fulvio Cerutti—and shocked everyone by remaining happily married for thirteen years until her death in 1995.

"My honeymoon has never ended," the ninety-five-year-old Pia announced after celebrating her tenth wedding anniversary in 1992. "The fact that he's sixty-six years my junior doesn't affect our happiness. We're living proof that in love, age doesn't matter. Many people thought I was crazy to marry Fulvio. But I didn't pay any attention to them and I've never regretted it."

In 1982, Pia, a millionairess, and Fulvio, an Italian nobleman, fell in love after meeting in a lawyer's office in the town of Omegna, Italy. When they married several months later, many people

63

were suspicious that Fulvio, despite his background, was after Pia's real estate fortune. When the couple walked down the street, townspeople would curse and jeer Fulvio.

"For most people it was impossible to believe love could blossom between a young man and a woman old enough to be his great-great-grandmother," he admitted. "But our love was stronger."

According to Italian news accounts back then, Pia lived in a leaky run-down villa. Although she was a millionairess, she ate mostly bread and cheese because she just didn't have the heart to cook decent meals or fix up her home. She was a lonely and desperate woman whose worldly goods were going to ruin. But all that changed when Fulvio entered her life.

"I've stopped thinking about my age completely, and now I'm going out and doing things I haven't done in years," Pia declared. "Fulvio made me feel young again. I've even changed my looks. Now I wear high heels and go to the beauty parlor often."

After their marriage, the couple traveled to Alaska, Argentina, and Japan. "While we were in Japan, we went out every night," Fulvio recalled. "We even went to a disco and Pia and I danced until the wee hours of the morning. She was tireless."

Over the years, the townspeople who considered Fulvio a gold digger have changed their tune, said Father Giovanni, the parish priest. "I believe their marriage is working much better than that of many other couples," he said in 1992.

Fulvio's sixty-four-year-old mother and seventy-four-year-old father became good friends with Pia. Her sixty-three-year-old niece even calls Fulvio "Uncle."

In a newpaper interview after their tenth anniversary, Pia said the couple's love was stronger than ever. They spent quiet evenings holding hands. She played the piano for him while he cooked for her.

"At bedtime, Fulvio caresses me and gives me little kisses," she said at the time. "I always fall asleep in his arms and awake the next morning the same way. These have been ten glorious years—the best years of my life."

Pia died in 1995 of a heart attack at the age of ninety-eight.

Mud Hut Romances

In 1993, Cheryl Mason was an English housewife with three children. Two years later, she had given up that life for one as the wife of a Masai warrior living in a mud hut in Africa.

"I know a lot of people look down on me, thinking it's scandalous to leave your husband and children for a warrior tribesman, but I was deeply in love," Cheryl told the English press, which had a field day publishing stories about the wild romance.

In November 1993, Cheryl, then thirty-three, met twenty-four-year-old tribesman Daniel Lekimencho while she was on vacation in Kenya with a girlfriend. He and other Masai warriors had come to the hotel to perform a tribal dance for the guests.

It was love at first sight.

"I was captivated by his powerful yet elegant movements," she recalled. "I knew instantly I had to be his wife."

She talked with Daniel who invited her back to his village. Cheryl said she was horrified at what she saw. "Flies were everywhere. People lived in little igloo-shaped mud huts stuck together with cow dung. But Daniel and I grew so much at ease that I felt as if we'd known each other in another life. For the entire three weeks of my vacation, we were never apart. I'd lie in his arms at night thinking, 'I'm the girl from the church choir. This can't be real.'"

Cheryl returned to England and asked for a divorce from her husband. "I'd been bored out of my mind in my marriage," she said. After she broke the news to her three children, Cheryl went back to Africa to live as a Masai warrior's wife even though they were not married.

"I slept on the dirt floor of our hut," Cheryl recalled. "I waited on Daniel hand and foot—which I adored doing, even though I'd refused to pick up my husband's socks."

In November 1994, she returned to England with Daniel so she could be closer to her children. Once the divorce came through, she and Daniel were married in traditional Masai dress. "This love was too powerful to ignore," declared Cheryl.

❤ ❤ ❤

Lonely British divorcée Betty Taylor went on a safari in Kenya to get over the breakup of a lengthy relationship and returned home with a new husband—a native half her age who lived in a mud hut.

"Romance was the last thing on my mind when I went on vacation," fifty-six-year-old

Betty told the press in Kent, England, where she introduced her spouse, twenty-five-year-old Said Said to shocked family and friends. "Now I have a husband ten years younger than my daughter Bridie. I'm happier than ever."

Said, who was living in a mud hut with six other people, says he fell in love with Betty the moment he saw her walk out of the fancy Plaza Beach Hotel in Mombasa. They struck up a friendly conversation.

Betty thought Said was just a beach boy trying to sell souvenirs to a gullible tourist. But in no time she had fallen for his simple native charms. "I was a bit wary at first," she recalled. "But then we got to talking and he turned out to be a perfect gentleman."

The Wedding without the Groom

When Carrie Gallmeyer remarried her ex-husband Louis, there was only one thing missing—the groom. He was eight thousand miles away.

Yet the marriage was perfectly legal.

Louis and Carrie's first marriage to each other lasted only seventeen months. Soon after their divorce in 1989, the pair realized they missed each other terribly. So they rekindled their love, even though Louis, a marine, was stationed in North Carolina and she was living in Florida.

"We were so miserable being apart that we got re-engaged in 1990 when Louis was home on leave," Carrie recalled. "We had our hearts set on saying our vows on November 28—the same date we got married in 1987—because we didn't want to have two wedding anniversaries."

But three months before their planned wedding, Louis phoned Carrie from North Carolina with disappointing news: He was being shipped to the Middle East in seventy-two hours, where he would serve aboard the USS *Guam* in the Persian Gulf—a region about to erupt into war.

"I didn't know whether I would be his wife or his widow," Carrie said. "But we made up our minds that nothing was going to stop us from getting married on our anniversary—not even the threat of war or the fact that he couldn't be with me to say 'I do.'"

So Carrie arranged a proxy marriage with the approval of the Broward County (Florida) clerk. Louis signed a blank marriage certificate and sent a letter giving permission for Carrie's best friend, Ellen Monaco, to stand in for him during the wedding at the home of Carrie's parents in Sunrise, Florida.

Because the father of the bride was a notary, he conducted the ceremony as Carrie stood next to the honorary groom. Then Carrie and her real husband attended separate celebrations eight thousand miles apart.

"I was there for the first ceremony and it didn't turn out too well," said Louis. "Maybe my not being there will change our luck."

Gender-Bending Bride and Groom

A German couple who each underwent successful sex-change operations wed each other in 1993, according to European publications.

The bride, Frieda, was once a he and the groom, Martin, was once a she.

The couple agreed to talk to the press only if their real names and the location of their home were kept secret.

"I know that our future as husband and wife will not be easy, but I'm confident that our love is stronger than any prejudice," declared Martin, a twenty-four-year-old carpenter who was born a petite girl named Maria.

As a youth, Maria was a tomboy who always felt more like a boy than a girl. In her late teens, psychologists examined her and recommended sex-change surgery so that Maria was transformed into Martin.

Meanwhile, Frieda suffered a similar period of sexual confusion as a young man named Fritz who sported a mustache and goatee. But when he was in his twenties, he had a sex-change operation and became Frieda.

"When I first met Martin [in 1991], I immediately felt he was the man with whom I could build my new life as a woman," said Frieda, a twenty-six-year-old computer operator. "But when we started going together, people treated us as if we were suffering some terrible contagious disease. It had already been impossible for some people to accept my sex change—and the fact that I was going out with a man who used to be a woman was even worse.

"Nobody seemed to understand that Martin and I were simply born in the wrong bodies."

Said their priest, who blessed their union, "I only wish all the other so-called 'normal' couples of my parish were so pure and loving as Martin and Frieda."

And the Groom Wore a Lovely Gown

At the 1992 marriage of Bruce Laker, thirty-six, and Vanda Young, forty, on England's Isle of Wight, the bride wore the tux and the groom wore the dress.

As a university researcher, Bruce was fascinated at how easy it was to pass himself off as a woman simply by donning women's apparel. He noticed that people reacted differently toward him when he wore a dress. Because his students were leery of his findings, he bet them that he could trick anyone into believing he was a woman. After they accepted his challenge, Bruce slipped into a sexy outfit and went to a disco. He played his female role so convincingly that by the end of the evening, a male disc jockey was begging him for a date.

Bruce decided that the ultimate test would be to play the role of the bride at his wedding. And, for whatever reason, Vanda agreed.

When they applied for their marriage license, Bruce confessed to the clerk, "There's one thing I must mention: I will be the one wearing the wedding dress."

The clerk frowned and asked for legal advice because the law states that due solemnity must be observed at weddings. The official word came back that the couple could wed in the clothes of their choice—as long as they took their marriage vows seriously.

"Don't get the wrong idea," Bruce told reporters later. "I'm not a transvestite. I'm a normal heterosexual man. It's all a matter of research."

❤ ❤ ❤

After sixty-four years of marriage, Alfred and Anita Lehde staged a second wedding ceremony—only this time, he looked like the bride and she looked like the groom.

As if that wasn't wacky enough, everyone in the wedding ceremony followed the bride and groom's example. The men dressed as women and the women dressed as men.

In 1986 at the Good Samaritan Home in St. Louis, nearly one hundred family members and friends sang "Here Comes the Bride" as eighty-six-year-old Alfred and eighty-five-year-old Anita marched down the aisle. They were greeted by friend Gladys Pfaff, who put on a fake mustache before officiating at the ceremony.

The couple's marriage vows were quite different from the ones they exchanged back in 1922 when they first got married. During their second time around, they promised to keep charges on their credit accounts below the four-hundred-dollar mark and never stay out late.

Said the blushing, uh, groom, "We did it just for fun."

Better Late than Never

She Finally Got Her Man

Eluned Griffiths dumped boyfriend Basil Tite at her mother's insistence—and never stopped regretting it.

So sixty years later, Eluned tracked down Basil—the only man she ever loved—and ended up marrying him.

Eluned, from Wales, and Basil, an Englishman, began dating in 1931 when they both were in their twenties and lived in West Yorkshire, England. "We were very much in love and I was in seventh heaven," recalled Eluned, a retired teacher. "But my mother—a devout Welsh Congregationalist—didn't approve because Basil was English and a Christian Scientist. She made me come back to Wales [in 1932] and I lost all contact with Basil."

Basil eventually married someone else, had three children and became a widower in 1992 after fifty-six years of marriage. Eluned never wed—and never forgot Basil.

In 1992, at the age of eighty-three, Eluned decided to try and find her long-lost lover. So she advertised in a magazine for retirees. She sent a picture of Basil as a young man to the publication with a plea for him to contact her.

A friend of Basil spotted the picture and mailed it to him. The flattered Basil wrote to Eluned and the two exchanged a string of passionate love letters. Months later, they wed in Eluned's tiny village in Wales. "Our wedding day was the happiest day of my life," beamed Eluned. "My biggest regret is that I didn't marry Basil when I was a girl. I should never have listened to my mother."

❤ ❤ ❤

Another British couple took sixty years to get married.

Back in 1931, Mary Swithenbank and John Talbot were ten-year-old playmates in the London suburb of Harrow when they staged a pretend wedding. "I had a veil and a bunch of flowers," Mary recalled. "John took my arm as the groom. John's little brother Peter and my younger sister Betty were our attendants. They were both six."

As teenagers, John and Mary fell in love and became engaged the night before he went off to fight in World War II. But three days before the planned wedding in 1943, John called it off. "I was devastated," said Mary. "I hated him. I told my friends I never wanted to see him again."

After the war, in 1946, Mary wed Albert Townsley and ten years later they struck up a friendship with John and his wife, Ivy. They went to each other's parties and exchanged Christmas and birthday cards. John and Mary never mentioned their 1943 breakup.

Mary's husband died in 1988 and two years later, John's wife did too. One day, John visited Mary—and the embers started to flame. In 1991, they got hitched with John's brother Peter and Mary's sister Betty as their attendants—just like in the couple's mock wedding sixty years earlier.

The Second Time Around—Forty Years Later

After getting divorced, it took William and Lucille Durham forty years to figure out they still loved each other. So they finally were reunited as husband and wife, fulfilling the dreams of their four children, who all had roles in the wedding.

"I love Lucille today even more than the day we first married," seventy-five-year-old William told reporters at the reception. Gazing into the eyes of his seventy-three-year-old bride, he gushed, "She's the only gal in the world for me. I get down on my knees every night and thank God for this wonderful second chance for our love."

The couple split in 1945 after fifteen years of marriage. Lucille admitted that she and William squabbled over silly things and finally decided to call it quits. She raised their four children alone.

The kids lost touch with their father. But then, in 1975, after hearing some friends talk about their dads on Father's Day, Walter, the youngest member of the Durham family, decided to track down his dad through a great-aunt.

"Dad was living in Beloit, Wisconsin, so I phoned him and then flew to Beloit to meet him," recalled Walter from his home in Denver. "When I saw my dad, all the emotions that had been welling up inside me for so long came pouring out. We were hugging and crying at the same time, and I told him, 'We have so much lost time to catch up on, Dad.'"

At the time Lucille was living in Grand Rapids, Michigan. In 1984, she moved to Denver to live with Walter, who was a minister at the Church of God in Christ. Walter began playing Cupid.

"I kept urging Mom to call Dad," said Walter. "Finally she did. She admitted she was as nervous as a sixteen-year-old going out on her first date. She said her knees were wobbly and her heart was thumping so hard that she was afraid she'd fall on her face if she stood up."

William kept asking Lucille to come see him. She eventually caved in and in 1985, after he sent her plane fare, she flew to Beloit. "When I stepped off the plane, I spied him immediately," Lucille recalled. "His hair had turned gray, but I would have recognized him anywhere.

"My heart was in my throat. I was so choked up I could barely call his name. It had been forty years since we parted, but seeing him made it seem like only yesterday. It was as if we were two kids in love all over again."

Within days, William proposed. Lucille wasn't sure what to do, so she asked Walter for advice. Recalled her son, "I told her, 'Go ahead. You love him and he loves you. Let's be a family once again.'"

Lucille accepted William's proposal. They were married in the Church of God in Christ in Grand Rapids with all the kids taking part in the wedding. Son Walter performed the ceremony, daughter Peggy played the organ and was maid of honor, son Clyde sang a solo, and another son, William George, was best man. The couple's ten grandchildren also were in attendance.

"This time, it's for keeps," said Lucille. "I don't want to spend another forty years apart from the man I love."

Making an Honest Woman out of Her

For thirty-seven years, Gerrie Yancey hid the truth from her former paramour George Eiferman that he was the father of their love child.

After she finally confessed to him over the phone, George and Gerrie saw each other for the first time in thirty years. And four months later, they got married.

George and Gerrie first fell for each other at California's Venice beach in 1955. He was twenty-nine years old and the proud owner of several muscle-man titles and she was a thirty-three-year-old professional singer. "It was love at first sight," recalled George.

But there was a problem. Gerrie was married to Warren Yancey and had a daughter, so George and Gerrie didn't reveal their true feelings for each other. Instead, George became friends with the Yanceys. However, later that year, Gerrie and Warren got divorced.

When Gerrie and George saw each other again, they let loose their passion for each other. "When he walked in, I was in ecstasy," recalled Gerrie. "I had never dreamed that he felt the same way. We fell into each other's arms. It was a very torrid afternoon."

A month later, Gerrie discovered she was pregnant with George's baby. But before she could tell her lover the news, Warren walked back into her life. "We decided to get married again for the good of the family," she said. "He knew the child wasn't his, but he agreed to raise him as his own.

"I couldn't tell George either. I didn't want to make him feel an obligation. I thought it was best for everyone concerned if I kept the secret from George." Nine months after her affair with George, Gerrie gave birth to a son she named Bob.

George still remained friends with the Yanceys and even played with baby Bob, not knowing that the infant was really his own son.

George went on to win the Mr. Universe title in 1962 and became a fitness trainer to such stars as Debbie Reynolds and Ryan O'Neal. He also got married.

But Gerrie never stopped pining for George. Eventually, when Warren died and George had divorced his wife, Gerrie decided it was time for her old flame to know the truth. So in 1992 she called George at his gym in Las Vegas and talked to him for the first time in over thirty years.

Recalling how she broke the startling news to George, Gerrie said, "George, are you sitting down? Do you remember tossing little Bob in the air when he was a baby? Well, he isn't Warren's son. He's yours!'"

George was so dumbfounded that he couldn't speak at first. When he finally collected his thoughts, he asked his long-lost sweetheart to marry him! And she accepted!

But she warned him that she was no longer the young woman she once was—she was now seventy years old. But George reminded her that he had grown older too and was now sixty-six—although still in tip-top physical shape.

The weight lifter rushed to Gerrie's California home and when she opened the door, he took her in his arms. "He must have kissed me for fifteen minutes," she recalled. "My lips were sore for days."

Said George, "I never stopped loving her. The excitement I felt on that encounter so many years ago has never gone away."

Four months after that incredible call, Gerrie and George were wed—with their son Bob looking on. Said Gerrie, "True love never dies."

Love Lost and Found

Plagued with regret over passing up the love of her life twenty-six years earlier, Marie Tumaniszwili hired a private detective to get her old boyfriend Iztok Djordjevic back.

Incredibly, it worked. Months after they were reunited, the two got married.

Their love story began back in 1965 when Marie, then eighteen, and Iztok, then twenty-five, met in a cafeteria at the University of Hartford in Connecticut. After a year of dating, they talked about marriage. But Marie's father squelched the romance. He feared that Iztok, a student of music and languages, wouldn't be able to support her properly.

Without revealing that her father had put the kibosh on the relationship, Marie tearfully bid her beau adieu—even though she felt she had given up her true love. Heartbroken, Iztok warned Marie that she was making a terrible mistake. They kissed one last time and left each other's lives for the next twenty-six years.

In the intervening years, Marie married a man who her father had chosen for her and she bore him three children. Iztok also married and had two kids. Marie and Iztok each divorced their spouses after twelve years of marriage.

Marie never forgot Iztok. In 1991, after years of living alone with her children and running a kennel business in Brooksville, Florida, the forty-four-year-old woman spotted an ad for a private eye. She hired Bob

Stewart of the Pasco Detective Agency in nearby Hudson, Florida, for $250 to find her former sweetheart. "What could I lose?" Marie recalled.

"All I had was Iztok's name and the fact that he once lived in the Mystic–New London area of Connecticut. The detective said, 'Don't get your hopes up.' Then he called to say he located five hundred families with that surname."

Marie thought the search would prove futile. But a month later, the detective called her with the news she had longed to hear. "Bob said, 'I found him. And the best part is that he's not married.' I was absolutely floored."

Stewart found Iztok, fifty-one, in Stamford, Connecticut, where he was teaching languages. When Iztok learned that his former flame was looking for him, he immediately called her.

Ten days after their first phone call in twenty-six years, Iztok flew to Florida to embrace Marie. "It was very romantic," she recalled. "He captured my heart all over again. It was an instant re-falling in love."

Incredibly, just six hours after their airport reunion, the pair were engaged. They wed several months later.

"When the story hit the papers, I got deluged by people wanting me to find their lost loves," recalled Stewart. "Over the next year I brought eighty-eight couples together. But no case was as nice and touching as Marie's and Iztok's. What a great ending."

Legal at Last

The nine kids loved their mom and dad very much. There was only one thing the youngsters wished their parents would do—get married.

So the kids hatched a plan for getting them hitched. And to their joy, it worked.

In 1981 in Smethwick, England, Rod Wotenick and Denise McDonald fell in love and moved in together. They started a family—which grew by the year—but the couple never got around to tying the knot. Finally, in 1993, the kids launched a campaign to get their unmarried parents to wed. Plotting the conspiracy were Lisa, 11; Kerri, 10; Luke, 9; Emma, 8; Bluw, 6; Dawn, 5; twins Faye and Kim, 3; and Tracey, 2.

The crusade featured everything from phony wedding bands to a bridal bouquet and outright begging—and it worked like a charm.

In the presence of his parents, Luke constantly whistled "Here Comes the Bride." Recalled Luke, "After a while, it really irritated Mom and Dad, especially if they were watching TV."

Kids would ask their thirty-five-year-old father such questions as "What's a best man?" "What's a honeymoon?" The younger children began calling their thirty-four-year-old mother "Mrs. Mommy."

To hammer home their point, several of the children began wearing handcrafted wedding rings made of gold candy wrappers.

When Lisa learned that a school friend of hers was a bridesmaid in a wedding, Lisa asked for and received her friend's bouquet. "I took the bouquet home and carried it around the house," Lisa recalled. "I said, 'Mom, don't you think I'd make a wonderful bridesmaid?'"

81

After months of the kids hinting around, Lisa wrote a big note that read, MOM AND DAD, WILL YOU GET MARRIED? All the kids signed it and left it in the kitchen. When Denise saw the note, she burst into tears. Rod was moved too.

"The kids' hints finally warmed us up to the idea of marriage," Denise said. "Rod and I fell into each other's arms and began making wedding plans.

"When we told the children, they went wild with joy, shouting, 'Hurray! We've done it! Mom and Dad are going to get married!'"

Denise and Rod exchanged vows in a quiet civil ceremony. When the newlyweds came home, the children were lined up in the yard, smiling and standing underneath a sign that read, CONGRATULATIONS, MOM AND DAD—LEGAL AT LAST!

Together at Last

In two strikingly similar cases, adoptees found their birth parents, brought them together again after three decades—and rekindled old fires.

Love triumphed in both cases when the parents walked down the aisle to become man and wife.

The real-life soap opera began in 1963 for Barbara Colvin, then twenty, and her college boyfriend Larry Kellem, then twenty-four, when the two discovered that Barbara was pregnant. Unable to face her strict Methodist parents, Barbara fled to the home of a relative and gave birth to a daughter she named Anya. After agonizing over what to do, Barbara and Larry agreed to give up the baby for adoption and go their separate ways.

Their daughter, Lauri Keller, was raised in a loving adoptive family. But Lauri had an enduring curiosity about her birth parents. So in 1991, Lauri, a San Diego marketing consultant, contacted the adoption agency. Barbara, twice-divorced mother of two and antique shop owner in Billerica, Massachusetts, had given the agency her name and address in case her daughter ever wanted to contact her. Barbara then received Lauri's phone number.

In February 1993, Barbara phoned Lauri and two weeks later, they met in San Diego. "We hugged and stared at one another," Barbara told reporters. She tracked down Larry, a divorced father of one and owner of a lawn sprinkler business in Upton, Massachusetts. He later visited Lauri.

Larry and Barbara then began talking on the phone to each other. "Something was happening," he admitted.

On July 4, 1993, Lauri met her birth parents for dinner in Boston and could see they were still in love. Eventually, Lauri encouraged them to date, which they did. "You two belong together," Lauri told them.

After the couple took a trip to Florida, Barbara phoned Lauri. "I heard it in her voice," recalled Lauri. "She said, 'It started again.' I knew then that they'd be together forever."

In the summer of 1995, Larry, fifty-six, and Barbara, fifty-two, got married—with Lauri as the bridesmaid. "This whole thing has been like a dream," Lauri told *People*. "I believe in my heart that they belong together. I knew the feelings were there. I just sort of stoked the flame."

The happy ending was almost identical to one experienced in 1992 by Jim and Dottie Craig and their daughter Jane Cole.

For Jane, an adoptee who reunited her parents after twenty-nine years and then spurred them to wed, "It's like a miracle out of a fairy tale."

In 1962, unmarried twenty-two-year-old Dottie Dyer became pregnant with Jane. Furious and ashamed, her strict parents sent her off to a home for unwed mothers to have her baby in secret.

"My boyfriend, Jim Craig, desperately wanted to marry me," recalled Dottie, of Peterborough, Ontario, Canada. "We wanted to keep our baby and start a life together. But my parents wouldn't let us." The baby was given up for adoption.

Jim and Dottie married other people, but stayed in touch over the years. Meanwhile, when their daughter, Jane, turned eighteen, she began searching for her parents. Eventually, she found her mother's name and called her up.

"As soon as Dottie heard my voice, she told me that she loved me and always had—and that she never wanted to give me up," recalled Jane. "I said, 'Mom, I love you.' And she said, 'I love you too.'"

Elated, Dottie called Jim with the happy news. By then, Jim's wife had died and Dottie's marriage had fallen apart. They got together to talk about their newfound daughter. Recalled Dottie, "Our love blossomed greater than ever."

After dating for a few months, Dottie and Jim decided to get married. They tied the knot in 1992 with Jane as the maid of honor. "Their wedding was the most beautiful day of all our lives," said Jane. "As I stood in church, I prayed, 'Thank you, God, for helping me find my mom and dad—and for helping them find each other again.'"

The 101-Year-Old Groom and His Blushing 95-Year-Old Bride

Sam Ackerman may have been 101 and his bride Eva Powers 95, but they acted like lovestruck teens when they tied the knot in their nursing home.

"Heck, just because we were born in the 1800s doesn't mean we've forgotten how to love each other like a couple of youngsters," Sam told reporters at his reception. "We're the happiest newlyweds in the world."

The two met in 1986 when Eva moved into the Dumont Masonic Home in New Rochelle, New York, where Sam already lived. Eva, then ninety-one, had been widowed for more than sixty-five years and was shy and lonely. "I stayed in my room because I'd been used to being alone all my life," she said.

Sam, then ninety-seven, a widower for thirty-one years and a retired clothing salesman, was still very active and sociable. One day, he appeared at Eva's doorway down the hall.

"I took her for a game of bingo," he recalled. "And that was the beginning of a romance made in heaven." They began spending all their time together, attending exercise class, art class, plays, and concerts. Sam nicknamed Eva "Cookie" because she used to cook in a restaurant.

In 1990, Sam's male roommate left. So Sam had an idea. After four years of dating Eva, he asked the nursing home officials if Eva could move in with him. But they said no because only married couples could live together. Sam figured that was no problem and asked Eva to marry him. She accepted.

A week later, they were wed with Eva's granddaughter as the maid of honor. "After a lifetime of struggling and being alone, suddenly I have a wonderful man to share my twilight years," Eva told her wedding reception guests.

Added Sam, "I say my prayers every day to God for bringing me the most beautiful woman on the face of the earth—my little Cookie."

The 119-Year Itch

Waldemiro Silva was in no hurry to get married. The Brazilian bachelor kissed his single life good-bye when he finally wed—at the ripe old age of 119!

On March 1, 1986, Waldemiro took fifty-seven-year-old Iracema Ladeira to be his bride in a ceremony followed by a large, rollicking reception.

"I've never loved anybody so much before in my life," he told guests. "I decided to make Iracema my wife in the eyes of God. I'm a really lucky man."

Waldemiro was born in 1866—before the completion of the first transcontinental railroad, the great fire of Chicago, the patent of Alexander Graham Bell's telephone, and General Custer's defeat at Little Bighorn. At the age of ten, Waldemiro was brought to Brazil from Africa as a slave. After slavery was abolished in 1888, he worked for the descendants of his former master, including the grandson, Edio Costa, in a clothing factory and on a farm near Rio de Janeiro.

Waldemiro never married. But in 1977, when he was 111, Iracema walked into his life. She was a widow hired as a maid in the Costa household.

"I knew from the beginning that she was my type of woman," Waldemiro told reporters. "But I didn't want to come on too strong. So in the beginning I just acted very cute and sweet, knowing that when I kissed her for the first time she would be unable to resist me."

Waldemiro began giving Iracema presents like candy or flowers. "One day he told me he had a very special surprise for me and asked me to close my eyes," she recalled. "Then he kissed me on the lips and we started hugging and kissing. One thing led to another and it wasn't hard to figure out that I really loved this man. I was conquered by his humbleness, his simplicity, and his charm."

After squiring Iracema for eight years, her 119-year-old boyfriend began considering marriage. "I started thinking that one day I'm going up to heaven and I just didn't want to be alone," Waldemiro recalled. So he got down on his knees and asked Iracema to marry him. She gave him a happy yes.

Their boss, Edio Costa, then threw a big wedding. The bride and groom were taken separately to Rio's St. George Brazilian Church in horse-drawn carriages, as hundreds of people lined the streets to salute Waldemiro.

Said Bishop Dom Hugo da Silveira Lino, who presided at the wedding, "Waldemiro is a living example that love and life know no time. You're never too old."

Wild and Wacky Weddings

A Family Affair

Four sisters and their brother all married their sweethearts—in the same ceremony!

"I haven't lost four daughters and a son," their father, Bertil Nilsson, told wedding guests. "I've gained four sons and a daughter."

In a small church in the Swedish village of Onnestad in 1987, the five Nilsson children—Ingela, 28; Ajneta, 25; twins Anne Christine and Eva Karina, 23; and their brother Jorjan, 26—all got hitched at the same time.

After the ceremony was over, the priest, Father Michael Anefur, announced, "All this is my fault."

That's because in the fall of 1986, Father Anefur had asked the oldest of the Nilsson girls, Ingela, and her live-in boyfriend, Erling Anderson, to consider getting married. "They had been living together for several years and had a three-year-old son and a one-year-old daughter," the priest recalled. "As I baptized the children, I told the parents it was about time they got married. I jokingly told them, 'You're frightened of marriage—admit it.'"

Ingela took Father Anefur's words to heart. "We [she and her sisters] all lived with our boyfriends, as do most young people in the village," she said. "None of us had ever really given marriage much thought. But then Father Anefur started explaining the importance of marriage to us."

Ingela and Erling talked it over and came to the conclusion that they should marry. A short time later, Ingela invited her three sisters, her brother, and their companions over for dinner. Recalled Ingela, "I announced, 'Erling and I are getting married. Who wants to join us?' I was stunned when they all said, 'Yes, that's a great idea. Why not?'"

The next day, Father Anefur got a phone call from Ingela telling him, "Erling and I aren't frightened of marriage. To prove it, we want to get married. And to save time, can you marry my brother and sisters too? We all want to take the plunge together."

The wedding date was set for June 19—the day before a Swedish holiday originally intended to celebrate fertility.

For the ceremony, the brides wore pink and white wedding gowns and the men wore white tuxedos.

"The wedding was very nerve-racking for me," admitted Father Anefur. "I was desperately hoping not to get the names mixed up." Even though he knew the family well, the girls all looked quite similar. During the rehearsal, he had them stand on pieces of paper with their names on them.

"It's hard work going through the wedding speech of 'Do you take this person?' and so on ten times, waiting for the 'I do' reply ten times over," said Father Anefur. "I began to think there was an echo bouncing around. But it was a happy wedding. The parents were laughing and crying at the same time."

More than two hundred people packed the tiny church while the rest of the village's one thousand residents stood outside and cheered the newlyweds after the ceremony. Each couple climbed into their own open horse-drawn carriage. Then, with five horsemen leading the way and waving white flags, they headed to the reception at the family farm.

During the party, where a huge wedding cake was topped with five little bridal couples, Gunnel Nilsson, the matriarch of the family, announced, "It's heavenly. I'm in mother's paradise!"

America's Trashiest Wedding

Dee and Pat Wilhems will be the first to admit that their wedding was trashy.

That's because they got married in the back of a garbage truck— and spent their wedding night in the county landfill.

"We thought it would be fun—and it was," said the bride shortly after her 1995 wedding in Hartford City, Indiana. "When our friends and family heard what we were going to do, they weren't all that surprised. They knew we were a little wacky and crazy."

The ceremony was perfectly fitting for Pat, thirty-nine, because he's a sanitation worker. Dressed in his blue garbageman's uniform and a tie, the groom stood proudly in the back of a cleaned-out and decorated garbage truck. The thirty-five-year-old bride joined his side. She was wearing a wedding gown and veil made of 130 white thirteen-gallon kitchen trash

bags fastened with a glue gun. "It was beautiful," beamed Dee. "I swear it looked like it was made out of silk. It cost me about eleven dollars in bags and ribbons."

With a hundred people standing next to the garbage truck, which was parked behind the couple's house, Mayor David Bennett officiated at the second marriage for each. At the reception, the bride and groom cut the wedding cake, which was topped by a toy garbage truck.

On their wedding night, they drove a motor home to the Jay County landfill in Portland, Indiana. "The landfill is a nice one because they cover the garbage immediately with dirt," said Dee. "So we brought out our champagne and spent the night there."

Added Pat, "The view from that mountain [of trash] is as good as Gatlinburg [Tennessee] and not as far away and expensive."

Early the next morning, the newlyweds were rudely awakened by workers at the landfill. Explained Dee, "Our motor home was blocking the exit and there were eight trash trucks waiting to get out."

When Love Runs Amuck

Love ran amuck for bride Diane Whaley and groom Robert Jackson. They said their "I do's" while standing knee-deep in a mud pit.

"It's everything I hoped it would be and a lot more than I ever expected," said Diane, twenty, after her filthy nuptials at Off Road Westover, a truck mud-racing track near Birmingham, Alabama.

The idea to exchange vows in the slop was Robert's. The twenty-year-old groom was fanatical about truck mud racing, spending many Sundays cheering the racers as they sloshed around the track. When he proposed to Diane, he suggested that they get married in the mud pit in the center of the track. To his surprise and delight, she said fine.

So in 1991, with two thousand fans hooting and hollering their congratulations, a convoy of ten pickup trucks drove the wedding party and their families to the pit. Diane, in a white wedding gown, and Robert, in a blue suit, were helped from the lead truck. They walked hand in hand into the mud and stood knee-deep in the mess about ten yards from the bank. Eight bridesmaids in formal dresses followed the couple into the muck and formed a semicircle around them.

Judge Tommy Snowdown, who performed the ceremony, wore rubber boots as he stood on the pit's edge. He conducted the ceremony while hooked up to a microphone so the racing fans could hear.

When the ten-minute ceremony ended, the crowd roared its approval. Then two pickups raced into the pit, spraying muddy water over the entire wedding party. While the bridesmaids frolicked in the slop, guests joined in and showered the newlyweds with mud and beach toys. The muddy and drenched couple then sloshed their way to a reception in the track's main clubhouse.

"I know it's weird, crazy, and outrageous," Diane told reporters, "but I love him. In some ways, this is more special than a church wedding."

The World's First Virtual Wedding

Monika Liston married Hugh Jo in a palace in the Lost Continent of Atlantis.

For real. Sort of. They became the world's first couple to get married in a virtual reality wedding. And it was all perfectly legal.

Monika, twenty-five, and Hugh, thirty-three, had planned to elope. But a friend at Cyber-Mind VR Center in San Francisco, where Monika works, suggested that the couple become cyber-space pioneers by getting married in VR, or virtual reality. In VR, you wear a wraparound head-mounted monitor and hold a handheld controller. What you see is another world—a computer-generated environment. By moving your head and operating the controls, you can move your VR counterpart.

"When I first considered a VR wedding, I thought it was a crazy idea," admitted Monika. "But after talking it over with Hugh, we decided it would be something so memorable and different that it would be fun. We'd be the first to ever try this."

The couple then had to figure out what virtual reality they wanted to get married in. "We could be anything and be anywhere we wanted," said Monika. "We could be monsters or blobs or aliens and we could make up any world—limited only by our imagination. We wanted a place where no one could possibly get married in real life. We came up with Atlantis because it doesn't really exist."

Monika's colleagues called contacts in the VR industry to help tailor the computer pro-gramming necessary to recreate the lost continent and to fit the needs of the ceremony. "Hugh and I worked on the storyboards," said Monika. "I wanted it to be romantic and come riding into Atlantis on a horse."

For the actual wedding, which took place at CyberMind in 1994, about three hundred guests showed up to watch the VR ceremony on three large TV screens. "Because we were dealing with something new in cyberspace, I didn't want to wear the traditional white wedding dress," said Monika. "So I wore a silver gown and Hugh wore a pseudo-military outfit like that worn in *Star Trek*."

The bride and groom and minister each stood twelve feet from each other (to avoid VR interference) and then donned their monitored helmets. Seconds later they were in the VR world of Atlantis.

As the wedding guests watched on the TV screens, Monika rode in a horse-drawn chariot and picked up her husband by a bridge leading into Atlantis. The couple passed through its gates and disembarked at a palace. Inside, they approached the minister at the altar, and the actual wedding ceremony began.

When he pronounced them husband and wife, the couple gave each other a cyberkiss while hearts, flowers, and doves swirled around them. At the end of the VR ceremony, the couple took off their head monitors and walked over to each other where they exchanged real kisses and rings.

"We were concerned what our older relatives would think," said Monika. "But we explained everything to them beforehand. I don't know if they quite comprehended it all, but afterwards they said it was great.

"In many ways it was a traditional wedding. It's just that the environment was simulated." So, too, was one of their wedding gifts. A friend gave them a virtual reality iron and ironing board for their virtual reality chores.

Love Was in the Air

John and J. Len Lauersdorf put down roots—by getting married up in a tree.

The couple met in 1984 in a tree while both were working for a tree care company in Ravenna, Ohio. They started dating and soon fell in love.

One day, while discussing their wedding plans, J. Len blurted out, "I've got it! We'll get married in a tree. That's where we met, that's where we fell in love, and that's where we work."

For the wedding, the bride and groom, wearing hard hats, were perched fifty feet above the ground and secured by safety ropes. Down below, Ravenna Mayor Donald Kainrad performed the 1987 ceremony by shouting up to the couple. "It went great," John recalled. "Neither one of us was afraid of falling. But I was nervous about the possibility of dropping the ring."

❤ ❤ ❤

The Bride and Vroom

Marriage was a drag for Pascal and Veronique Dragotto. They capped their wedding with a breathtaking body slide—while being dragged by a race car at over 120 miles an hour.

The newlyweds were professional stunt performers who exchanged vows at the Castellet race track in Saint Zacharie, France, in 1991. Both were dressed in traditional wedding attire—but the material was superstrong so it could withstand the stunt.

After they completed the ceremony, Pascal, twenty-two, and Veronique, twenty-three, donned safety helmets and pads as added protection. Pascal then lay on his stomach and grabbed hold of a trapezelike bar connected to the back of a race car. The bride lay down on top of the groom's back and held on.

With a crowd cheering them on, the newlyweds waved and blasted down the track at spark-spraying speeds. After dragging the couple for nearly a mile, the car, which was driven by Pascal's father, came to a stop. The bride and groom then stood up and dusted themselves off as the spectators went wild. Although it was the first time that the couple had attempted the stunt together, they pulled it off without any injuries.

When asked why they attempted the dangerous body slide, Veronique replied, "We met each other doing stunt work, so what better way to begin our life together than with a joint performance?"

❤ ❤ ❤

Love on the Run

During the 1992 Los Angeles Marathon, Lorin Johnson, a thirty-year-old flight attendant, and Peter Elkin, a thirty-five-year-old real estate consultant, ran the first half of the race. Then they stopped just long enough to exchange their vows and then rejoined the marathon.

Before the race, Lorin and Peter, both experienced runners, enjoyed a wedding-day breakfast of a banana and a high-energy bar. The bride wore a white knee-length veil and a specially made lace dress designed for maximum movement and minimum moisture. The groom wore black shorts and a tuxedo T-shirt. With the bride carrying a bouquet of pink silk roses, the couple joined thousands of other runners and headed off on a memorable twenty-six-mile jaunt.

Flanked by twelve members of the wedding party, the two ran the course side by side, kissing along the route to the delight of the crowd. After running thirteen miles, the bride and groom stopped at the wedding

area on Hollywood Boulevard. Peter slipped into a tuxedo jacket and Lorin traded her running veil for a longer bridal veil. At the ceremony, officiated by fellow marathoner the Reverend Tim Egan, the couple exchanged rings and vowed devotion "in times of health and in times of sports injury."

After what Egan called "the most meaningful rest stop of their lives," the newlyweds returned to the race, finishing in five hours and thirteen minutes—their slowest time ever. "You can't hurry love," remarked a friend.

❤ ❤ ❤

Burning Love

In 1984, Ralph Deal, a firefighter in Statesboro, Georgia, asked his sweetheart, Cheryl, to marry him in a blazing building that the fire department had used in the past for practice drills. She agreed.

"I thought it would be more memorable to include my fellow firemen and give Cheryl a better idea of what I do for a living," Ralph explained to the press.

The couple dressed in fireproof suits and hats—Cheryl even wore a fireproof veil—and then entered the burning building where they exchanged their vows amid the heat and flames. After they were pronounced husband and wife, Ralph kissed his bride and then helped his partners put out the fire.

❤ ❤ ❤

99

Love Runs Deep

Ann Taylor and Rocky Davis had such deep feelings for each other that they got married 2,140 feet underground.

The couple wore traditional wedding outfits, but accessorized them with hard hats and steel-toed boots.

Rocky was waiting with the rest of the wedding party when the bride began the three-minute elevator ride to the base of Jim Walter Resources no. 5 mine in Tuscaloosa County, Alabama. Ann, who had to struggle to hold her gown down because of the shaft's updraft, was greeted by guests whistling the wedding march. Except for a minor glitch—Ann was wearing two left boots—everything ran smoothly.

She told reporters that she laughed for three days when Rocky, a miner, told her where he wanted to get married. After giving it careful thought, Ann agreed, considering the marriage in the mine an adventure.

Walking Down the (Grocery) Aisle

When Valerie Moutier and Jon Horne got married, they strolled down the aisle—the cheese aisle of a grocery store where they first met.

In 1994, Valerie was shopping at H.E.B.'s Central Market, in Austin, Texas, when a mutual friend introduced Jon to her while they stood in front of the cheese aisle.

"We began talking about good cheese and wine," she recalled. "Then we walked over to the wine section and began sampling good wines with good cheeses. When we finished shopping, I invited him over to my house for margaritas."

Their hearts melted for each other like Brie on a hot summer day. About six months later, they decided to get hitched where they met—in the cheese aisle. The store agreed, but asked the couple to keep the guest list down to about twenty people.

"We had a lot more friends than that so we told them to come and pretend they were shopping," Valerie recalled. Amid well-wishers, startled shoppers, balloons, and cheese wheels, the couple exchanged their vows.

"We wanted to do something fun," explained Valerie, a French artist. "We are not traditional people."

❤ ❤ ❤

Love's a Funny Thing

For her wedding outfit, bride Peggy Martin donned a mop of orange curls, big floppy shoes, a baggy, striped jumpsuit, and a shiny red nose. Groom Dale Harris wore a silly hat, white-face, a bulbous nose, and goofy, baggy clothes.

And that's the way the sixty-two-year-old great-grandmother and her fifty-nine-year-old beau wanted it. "We'd both had serious ceremonies for our first marriages—and those didn't work out," explained Dale. "So we wanted this wedding to be pure fun."

After divorcing her first husband, Peggy had taken up part-time clowning, performing at nursing homes and parades as "Ding-a-Ling." Wanting companionship, Peggy placed a personal ad seeking a tall, strapping, long-haired man—a "Grizzly Adams type."

Peggy, a St. Paul insurance company supervisor, dated each man who answered her. "The first nineteen were definitely not for me," she recalled. The twentieth man was Dale—a short, slightly-built, bald security guard. They soon fell for each other. Peggy taught Dale to clown and he became known as "Socker." When she accepted his marriage proposal, they decided to marry in 1995—at the twenty-first annual Midwest Clown Convention.

In front of guests sporting funny hats and a six-foot, three-inch male "flower girl," the clownish couple exchanged their vows. When the judged asked, "Do you, Ding-a-Ling, take Socker as your husband?" Peggy replied, "I certainly do!" amid honking horns.

Then, to symbolize their fun-loving wedding, Socker placed an eight-*carrot* ring on Ding-a-Ling's white-gloved finger.

❤ ❤ ❤

Pawesome Weddings

At the nuptials between Robert Engesser and Patricia Flair, the best man was a 155-pound black panther named Satan and the maid of honor was a 55-pound lioness cub named Tasheta.

"The animals are our best friends," Robert explained to the press after their 1984 wedding in Nashville. "That's why we decided to have them by our side."

Robert was the director of the Endangered Species, an organization which breeds and raises lions, tigers, panthers, and other animals on the endangered list. He and his parents, who founded the organization, traveled the country putting on exhibitions. Shortly after Patricia came to work for the group, she and Robert began dating.

Because of their love for animals, it was an easy decision to include the big cats in their wedding. At one point during the ceremony, six-month-old Tasheta playfully nibbled at Patricia's gown. When the couple were pronounced husband and wife, Tasheta led out a roar of approval and gave her mistress an affectionate lick.

Meanwhile, Satan let his feelings be known too—by rolling on his back and kicking all four paws in the air.

♥ ♥ ♥

A Date to Remember

June 19 is a special date for the Snellenberger family. Eight couples over three generations have married on that day.

The tradition was started in 1926 by Revell and Floy Snellenberger. Their four children followed in their footsteps and so did their three grandchildren.

In 1991, all the happily-married Snellenbergers gathered in Clay City, Indiana, home of Revell and Floy, retired dairy farmers. They had come to celebrate their anniversaries together—Grandma and Grandpa's 65th, Kenneth and Betty's 42nd, Loretta and Bob Wellman's 40th, Cletus and Carol's 35th, and Mazie and Jim Verden's 31st. It was also the wedding anniversary of Cletus's three children—Chris and Mary's 9th, Candis and Rusty Lavender's 6th, and Carey and Julie's 4th.

The family bash turned into a reunion for 150 relatives and friends from all over who came to celebrate the eight couples' anniversaries.

Although Revell and Floy were the first in the family to marry on June 19, their son Kenneth and daughter Loretta get credit for launching the tradition. When Kenneth decided to get married, he chose his parents' twenty-third anniversary to tie the knot.

"Our parents were so pleased that when it came my turn, I decided I wanted to get married on June 19th too," said Loretta. "After that, it became a tradition."

By 1995, Floy, eighty-six, proudly said that they had over 260 years of marriage among them without a divorce.

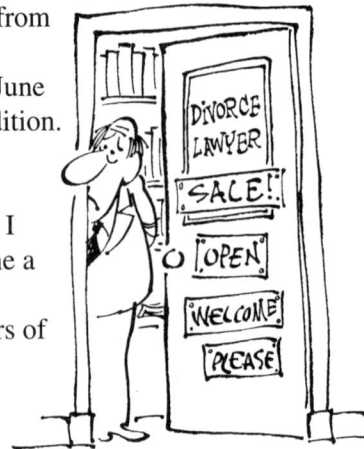